HS·AC

HOMELAND
OPERATIONAL ANA

Guidance on When to Estimate a Future Price Factor

Development of Criteria and
Thresholds

ISAAC M. OPPER, PRISCILLIA HUNT, LUCAS HUSTED, JESSIE COE, KATHRYN A. EDWARDS,
AARON STRONG, JEFFREY B. WENGER

This research was published in 2022.

About This Report

In 2017, Homeland Security Operational Analysis Center (HSOAC) researchers helped validate the Federal Emergency Management Agency's (FEMA's) cost estimates for rebuilding projects in Puerto Rico and the U.S. Virgin Islands (USVI) following Hurricane Maria. To estimate the costs to repair or replace a damaged facility (e.g., a school), FEMA uses a tool called the Cost Estimating Format (CEF). At a high level, the CEF is composed of the detailed line items necessary to do a repair (e.g., square feet of roofing and number of windows to be replaced) and adjustment factors for items, such as contingencies and geographic price differentials. For Puerto Rico and the USVI, another adjustment, called the future price forecast (FPF) factor, was included for the first time to capture economywide price increases directly related to the recovery effort. This was meant to capture the fact that investments that are large relative to the size of the economy drive up prices in general. To date, no guidance or criteria yet exist to help FEMA determine whether to apply an FPF in a future disaster.

The purpose of this report is to provide guidance to FEMA about when to estimate an FPF. This report focuses specifically on the price effects of disasters and the local conditions that influence an economic recovery from a disaster.

The findings in this report should be of interest to stakeholders involved in disaster-recovery activities, particularly those involved with FEMA's Public Assistance alternative procedures, in which FEMA gives a lump-sum payment for the rebuilding effort, rather than reimbursing the realized costs. Recipients of these payments can include include governments and local agencies, nongovernmental organizations, and the private sector. Furthermore, this report provides unique insights into the economics of disasters and should be of interest to researchers but also the larger community planning for or recovering from disasters.

This research was sponsored by FEMA and conducted within the Disaster Research and Analysis Program of the HSOAC federally funded research and development center (FFRDC).

About the Homeland Security Operational Analysis Center

The Homeland Security Act of 2002 (Section 305 of Public Law 107-296, as codified at 6 U.S.C. § 185) authorizes the Secretary of Homeland Security, acting through the Under Secretary for Science and Technology, to establish one or more FFRDCs to provide independent analysis of homeland security issues. The RAND Corporation operates HSOAC as an FFRDC for the U.S. Department of Homeland Security (DHS) under contract HSHQDC-16-D-00007.

The HSOAC FFRDC provides the government with independent and objective analyses and advice in core areas important to the department in support of policy development, decisionmaking, alternative approaches, and new ideas on issues of significance. The HSOAC FFRDC also works with and supports other federal, state, local, tribal, and public- and private-sector organizations that make up the homeland security enterprise. The HSOAC

FFRDC's research is undertaken by mutual consent with DHS and is organized as a set of discrete tasks. This report presents the results of research and analysis conducted under task order 70FBR218F00000141, Expert Analysis of FEMA Cost Estimate Development Process and Validation for FEMA-4340-DR-VI.

The results presented in this report do not necessarily reflect official DHS opinion or policy.

For more information on HSOAC, see www.rand.org/hsoac. For more information on this publication, see www.rand.org/t/RRA222-11.

Acknowledgments

We would like to thank our reviewers, James Hosek, Michael G. Mattock, and Erez Yerushalmi, for their very thoughtful comments and suggestions that improved the quality of this work. We are thankful for engineering and disaster-recovery expertise from Kelly Klima. We would also like to thank Jessie Riposo, who provided excellent leadership throughout the process. Last, we appreciate the time and effort made by the people who participated in expert workshops that informed this work, including RAND Corporation researchers R. J. Briggs, Joseph C. Chang, Samantha Cohen, Shelly Culbertson, Andrew Lauland, Robert J. Lempert, Bernd McConnell, Sean McKenna, Joshua Mendelsohn, Luke Muggy, John Plumb, M. Rebecca Kilburn, Shanthi Nataraj, Benjamin Lee Preston, Christopher M. Schnaubelt, and Kyle Siler-Evans.

Summary

The Federal Emergency Management Agency (FEMA) is increasingly interested in funding Public Assistance (PA) expenditures to help communities rebuild via fixed-price contracts, which provide lump-sum allotments to state, local, tribal, and territorial governments so that they can rebuild after natural disasters. Because these contracts cannot be renegotiated, both the local government and FEMA have a large incentive to estimate costs correctly before contracts are signed. Unanticipated increases in costs can leave a community with too little money to rebuild. Conversely, overestimating rebuilding costs can result in the federal government paying millions of dollars more than actual costs.

One challenge to providing an accurate estimate of construction costs is that the cost of rebuilding can be affected by the reconstruction effort itself. For example, if demand for construction increases and contractors find themselves bidding up their prices, constructing a building will be costlier after the disaster than it would have been before. One way to account for such changes is to use a future price forecast (FPF) factor, which adjusts a project's cost estimate to account for overall price-level increases caused by a disaster. However, no guidance or criteria yet exist to help FEMA determine whether to apply an FPF in a future disaster.

The purpose of this study was to help FEMA identify when to make a special provision for estimating future cost (or prices) to include in its Cost Estimating Format. That is, we sought to understand the conditions under which fixed-price forecasts are likely to underfund projects, thereby risking the completion of projects or financial stability of local governments, because of the medium-term effect on costs in the disaster-stricken area.

To carry out the study, we convened panels of experts to discuss scenarios of hypothetical disasters and, in particular, how these disasters could affect the local economies. We also tested a variety of community and disaster-related measures (e.g., labor supply issues for particular skills) that might be predictive of large cost increases and explored the relationship between different types of skills and labor-mobility variables (e.g., in- or out-migration) and disaster effects (e.g., fatalities, property damage) on construction costs. We then estimated how often disasters cause large increases (at least 10 percent) in construction costs and identified criteria to use in determining when an FPF might be warranted. We also explored the implications of these criterion thresholds by estimating FPFs in some "what-if" scenarios.

Key Findings

Motivated by expert scenario planning workshops, we tested a variety of community and disaster-related measures that might be predictive of large cost increases. We found strong support for the predictive power of two measures:

- **in-migration.** A county that has historically low in-migration is quite likely to see increases in its average construction wages after a large disaster; in contrast, an area with a high in-migration rate never sees a large increase, even after a large disaster.
- **disaster-related property damage.** Disasters of less than $1,000 per capita in damage (in fiscal year [FY] 2018 dollars) are highly unlikely to cause large cost increases (of 10 percent or greater), regardless of in-migration rate. However, between $1,000 and $10,000 per capita, the in-migration rate matters, and areas with low in-migration rates are more likely to have large disaster effects. Beyond $10,000 per capita, an FPF is probably warranted, although the data contain very few disasters with this level of damage, so whether it is $10,000 per capita or another number is not yet well known.

Although we found that few disasters cause large changes in average construction wages, wages in general are not particularly stable over time, and increases of more than 20 percent are not uncommon. The wide distribution of wage changes, although not necessarily related to a disaster, suggests that there is a lot of uncertainty in how much contractors are going to have to pay.

Recommendations

Given the economic and social costs of failing to use an FPF when one might be necessary, combined with the evidence of this study, we propose the following recommendations (all figures are in real 2018 dollars):

- If PA damage is **less than $1,000** (in FY 2018 U.S. dollars), do not estimate an FPF.
- If PA damage is **between $1,000 and $10,000** per capita (in FY 2018 U.S. dollars) and
  - the in-migration rate is less than or equal to 2.5 percent, estimate an FPF.
  - the in-migration rate is greater than 2.5 percent, do not estimate an FPF.
- If PA damage is **between $10,000 and $55,000** per capita (in FY 2018 U.S. dollars) and
  - the in-migration rate is less than or equal to 2.5 percent, estimate an FPF.
  - the in-migration rate is greater than 2.5 percent, conduct a preliminary analysis to determine whether estimating an FPF is warranted.
- If PA damage is **$55,000 per capita or greater** (in FY 2018 U.S. dollars), estimate an FPF.

Although there is no exact cutoff that predicts higher future costs with 100-percent accuracy, we recommend a lower bound of $1,000 per capita in damage. The scenarios predict that, if per capita damage is less than $1,000, the probability of a project needing an FPF is close to 0 (FPF estimate = 1.0).

For a disaster with per capita damage greater than $1,000 but less than $55,000, we recommend combining the damage threshold with a measure of in-migration to the community. For a disaster with per capita damage of $1,000 to $10,000, we recommend estimating an FPF for county-disasters with low in-migration; the implication here is that few of these county-disasters will need FPFs (FPF greater than 1.10) applied to project cost estimates. From the what-if scenarios, we learned that, for a county-disaster between $10,000 and $55,000 in per capita damage and high in-migration, there is a chance that it needs an FPF. This likelihood will be based on the scale and composition of the county's construction labor force and the price of labor, materials, and equipment in each of the PA categories (e.g., utilities).

Also as informed by the what-if scenarios, we added the recommendation of estimating an FPF at $55,000 per capita in damage regardless of in-migration rate. Our research shows that spending beyond $55,000 per capita (in FY 2018 U.S. dollars) leads to many market frictions and challenges in absorbing labor and capital that result in large price effects several years after a disaster. Very few disasters lead to this level of damage, so it would not be common and worth the trade-off.

Our assessment suggests that there is still a great deal of uncertainty in predicting the economic impacts of disasters. Therefore, we recommend that determining receipt of an FPF be a three-step process:

- In the first step, FEMA would determine whether the disaster meets predetermined thresholds to trigger the estimation of an FPF.
- If these trigger thresholds are met, FEMA would contract for an economic forecast for the region.
- If the forecast model anticipates future sustained costs in excess of 10 percent as a result of the disaster, the FPF factor would be adopted and used as part of the Cost Estimating Format.

Contents

CHAPTER SEVEN
Conclusions...39

APPENDIXES

Figures and Tables

Figures

Tables

CHAPTER ONE

Introduction

In the immediate aftermath of a natural disaster, two major economic shifts occur:

- a sudden loss in the region's factors of production (e.g., labor, materials, equipment) as people leave and physical capital is destroyed
- a sudden increase in the demand for construction labor, materials, and equipment as rebuilding commences.

Prevailing economic theory posits that both the reduction in supply and the increase in demand put upward pressure on construction costs in the region. However, a disaster's medium-run impact, which we define as the annual average effect during the five years postdisaster, is much less clear: Increasing wages spurred by the rebuilding process can lead people to migrate to the region or switch careers, either of which increases the supply of construction workers, but the disaster itself might cause others to reconsider building new structures in the area, which might not lead to increases in labor supply. This report focuses on ways to identify whether a disaster will cause increases in labor cost.

Background on Federal Emergency Management Agency Public Assistance Funding

Understanding how disasters affect the medium-term cost of construction is of crucial importance to the Federal Emergency Management Agency (FEMA), which finances much of any postdisaster rebuild. One reason is that FEMA is increasingly interested in funding Public Assistance (PA) expenditures via fixed-price contracts (often referred to as *alternative procedures*, or the *428 process*) rather than cost-plus contracts (standard procedures).[1] This greatly reduces the administrative burden on both FEMA and local governments because the fixed-price contracts allow the local government to call for competitive bids and shift the responsibility of cost management onto the construction firm. Additionally, local govern-

---

[1] *The 428 process* refers to Section 428 of Public Law 93-288, also known as the Robert T. Stafford Disaster Relief and Emergency Assistance Act, 1974, as added by Public Law 113-2, 2013, and codified at 42 U.S.C. § 5189f.

ments are provided more flexibility in how they rebuild and use any "excess" funds for hazard mitigation.

However, a fixed-price contract requires an accurate forecast of the cost (or price) of the rebuild. A systematic bias in cost forecasting that underpredicts costs would subject local governments to financial risk or risk that lack of funds will lead to a project not being completed. Conversely, a systematic bias resulting in overforecasting rebuilding costs would result in the federal government paying millions of dollars more than actual costs.

The Cost Estimating Format and a Future Price Forecast

To estimate the costs to repair or replace a damaged facility (e.g., a school), FEMA uses a tool called the Cost Estimating Format (CEF). At a high level, the CEF is composed of eight parts:

- Part A consists of an estimate to complete a public project (e.g., school, utility, road, bridge) based on parameters of the work order and U.S. average prices.
- Parts B through H consist of multipliers that can be applied to the part A estimate to adjust for factors influencing costs:
  - facilities and services
  - general conditions
  - design-phase contingencies
  - facility or project constructability
  - contingencies
  - access contingency
  - economies of scale
  - contractor overhead and profit
  - cost-escalation factor
  - permits and fees
  - applicant's reserve for change orders
  - architect and engineering design and project management.

Each of these has a set of criteria for which a FEMA cost estimator must determine whether a threshold has been met and therefore the multiplier is to be applied. Although some multipliers are single values that are turned on or off, other multipliers have ranges of values from which the cost estimator can select if a threshold is met.

After Hurricane Maria, another adjustment, called the future price forecast (FPF) factor, was developed.[2] An FPF was used for the first time for Puerto Rico and U.S. Virgin Islands (USVI) projects to capture economywide price increases directly related to the recovery

---

[2] We use the term *FPF* to refer to the estimate of how construction costs will increase due to a disaster. We use *FPF factor* to refer to the specific adjustment made to the CEF.

effort. Put another way, an FPF is intended to adjust a project cost estimate to account for overall price-level increases caused by a disaster. No guidance or criterion yet exists to help FEMA determine whether to apply an FPF in a future disaster.

What Is Already Known About Natural Disasters' Effects on Costs?

The literature on the economic impacts of natural disasters has grown tremendously in the past several decades.[3] Many analyses of the relationship between costs or prices and natural disasters have involved a case-study approach, focusing on a single event's impact. For example, six months after the 2010 earthquake in Chile, supermarket prices there had increased by approximately 2 percent (Cavallo, Cavallo, and Rigobon, 2014). Hurricane Katrina led to a 10-percent increase in housing prices in the two years following the storm (Deryugina, Kawano, and Levitt, 2018).[4] Other studies have used a more generalized approach with analyses of multiple disasters to estimate price responses. For example, Belasen and Polachek estimated that the average category 4 or 5 hurricane in Florida leads to a 4-percent increase in wages within the first four months after landfall (Belasen and Polachek, 2008). Murphy and Strobl found that the average hurricane leads to a 3- to 4-percent increase in housing prices after several years (Murphy and Strobl, 2010). Hurricanes Katrina and Rita's average effect was an 8-percent increase in wages after seven years (Groen, Kutzbach, and Polivka, 2020), and the average severe disaster leads to housing prices and rents that are lower by 2.5 to 5 percent (Boustan et al., 2020).

The existing approaches used in the literature do not allow an examination of the distribution of effects of previous disasters. The results from case-study analyses indicate that some disasters have large effects on prices, while others have minimal effects. The more generalized approach of estimating the average impact of a disaster focuses only on the distribution's first moment—the average effect. These approaches are not sufficient to answer questions about the shape of the distribution of effects. Additionally, the literature does not speak directly to the factors that influence whether the response to a given disaster falls in the upper tail of the distribution (e.g., severer disasters).

---

[3] See Botzen, Deschenes, and Sanders, 2019, for a review of the empirical literature on the economic impacts of natural disasters.

[4] Other examples include Abe, Moriguchi, and Inakura, 2014, in which the authors estimated that the 2011 Japan earthquake had only a modest effect on commodity prices, and Huerta-Wong et al., who found that the 2017 Mexico earthquake had no effect on food prices (Huerta-Wong et al., 2018).

Study Aim and Terminology

The purpose of this study was to help FEMA identify when to make a special provision for estimating future cost (or prices) to include in the CEF. That is, under what conditions are fixed-price forecasts likely to underfund projects, thereby risking the completion of projects or financial stability of local governments, because of the medium-term effect on costs in the disaster-stricken area? In this report, we provide further background on the following terminology: *price* and *costs*, *medium run*, and *large effects*.

Prices and Labor Costs

This report refers to prices because we consider an increase in aggregate construction costs to be an increase in aggregate prices under the assumption that a rebuilding project after a federally declared disaster is a necessity. Or, in economic terms, demand for reconstruction is relatively inelastic. In an ideal world, we would use the overall cost of construction or each of its component parts (material, equipment, and labor), but such data do not exist. In particular, there is no systematic data collection on capital (material and equipment) across jurisdictions at frequent intervals (e.g., annual); 2007 and 2012 data are available (U.S. Census Bureau, 2015). Labor data are available through the Bureau of Labor Statistics. As a result, we focus on labor costs. It is worth nothing that labor is a nontrivial, but not the major, component of construction costs. Cost shares for labor and capital across U.S. states (unweighted means) are 37 percent and 63 percent, respectively. Because labor is an important component of construction costs and might have barriers to mobility in the medium run, such as available housing in an affected area, we propose that the cost of labor is a good measure of a disaster's overall cost effects. That said, this measure might overstate the true rise in costs and result in conservative estimates of when a jurisdiction needs an FPF (i.e., more likely to indicate an increase in costs greater than 10 percent).

The Medium Run

We focus on the average effect over five years (starting the year after a disaster, to avoid short-run shocks of the emergency) for several reasons. First, a five-year span allows some time for recovery spending to flow into a region and for supply and demand for labor and capital to operate. Second, this period limits the impact of another disaster occurring in the region and affecting results. Third, on average, approximately 10 to 15 percent of all PA expenditures are incurred in each of the first five years following a disaster, at which point the per-year expenditures begin to slow down (U.S. Government Accountability Office, 2008).

Large Effects

FEMA currently allows for a 10-percent increase in construction cost in the CEF. Therefore, we focus on effects beyond the 10-percent threshold. This will help reduce the risk that a fixed-price contract will underpredict prices that would subject local governments to financial risk or risk of incomplete projects. Furthermore, based on the characteristics of the disaster and the region, we aimed to predict whether a given disaster will significantly increase construction wages.

Informing Our Analysis with Expert Workshops

Because there is little research on factors that contribute to large impacts of disasters, we convened panels of experts to explore possible correlates of large disaster effects for us to test (Hunt et al., 2020). We developed five catastrophic disaster scenarios and asked about potential long-term effects on the community:

- the Hayward earthquake, a major earthquake in the San Francisco Bay area in California
- the Circle earthquake, an earthquake in Circle, Alaska
- the fallout cauldron, a radiological event in Palm Beach and Miami, Florida
- black sky, an electromagnetic-pulse event in the Northeast
- Hurricane Kelly, a hurricane in Hawaii.

The key question during each workshop was what issues were considered in determining whether to use an FPF in the scenario. We identified a large list of county-level characteristics to test. For example, in all the workshops, experts thought that labor supply issues for particular skills could be problematic and raise costs. Therefore, we explored the relationship between different types of skills, labor-mobility variables, and disaster effects on construction costs. Further details of the methodology and results of these workshops are available from the authors.

The Structure of This Report

Chapter Two describes the measurement and data used for the analyses. This is followed by Chapter Three providing the methodology (maximum-likelihood method with Bayesian inference) to estimate a disaster's effect on aggregate costs and to estimate the correlation between variables of interest and cost effects; the correlated variables could then be used as criteria for when to use an FPF. Chapter Four provides the results of the cost effects of disasters, showing the extent to which disaster cause large cost effects (of 10 percent or greater). Using these findings, Chapter Five provides results of the relationship between variables of interest and cost effects. We then used the variables that are highly predictive of disaster effects (and therefore potentially good criteria) and, in Chapter Six, report on our assessment of thresholds that FEMA could use to determine whether to estimate an FPF. We finish the chapter with a subsection exploring the implications of particular thresholds by estimating FPFs in a variety of what-if scenarios by using a computable general equilibrium (CGE) model that was used to estimate an FPF in Puerto Rico. Chapter Seven concludes the report with an explanation of our findings and recommendations and directions for future research. The five appendixes provide more detail on the methodologies applied and the results of the study.

CHAPTER TWO

Data Description

This chapter provides details on the data used in the analyses. The first analytic decision is to determine what the appropriate level is (e.g., whether to analyze the data at the county level, at the state level, or at some other level of aggregation). On the one hand, we needed to analyze areas large enough to capture economic ties and the "full impact" of a disaster. On the other hand, analyzing areas that are too large runs the risk of finding no impact of the disaster on average wages in the entire region even when prices increase in the affected area within the larger region. Analyzing larger regions also complicates the way we determine a disaster's size. Is a hurricane that causes low-level damage throughout the Gulf Coast larger or smaller than one that causes large per capita damage in southern Florida but does not affect other areas in the region?

Given these questions, we considered multiple approaches. The state level appears to be too large in this respect because most natural disasters do not affect entire states and therefore would both introduce a lot of noise in estimating disaster effects and potentially miss import effects. Because so much of our raw data are at the county level, we cannot disaggregate our analysis any further than that. The question is then whether the analysis should be at an intermediate level, between states and counties. Possibilities include metropolitan statistical areas, the Bureau of Economic Analysis's (BEA's) economic areas, and the U.S. Department of Agriculture Economic Research Service's commuting zones and labor market areas. In our initial analysis, however, we found evidence that even conducting the analysis at these intermediate levels would cause us to understate the impact that disasters have on the regions' construction wages. See Appendix F for more information on this analysis. We therefore analyzed many correlates of wage effects throughout the country at the county level.

With that said, natural disasters do not respect this geographic distinction, nor do labor markets. Many disasters affect multiple counties—particularly neighboring counties—and potentially affect an entire region's labor market. As we discuss in Chapter Seven, this suggests that more work should be done to study the geographical scope of disasters' impacts.

The rest of this chapter is structured as follows: We first describe the main outcome of interest: cost of construction labor. We then describe data for the characteristics that are potentially correlated with disaster-related effects on costs, including disaster-specific information and county characteristics. The correlates of cost effects, which are observable either before or directly after a disaster, provide testable criteria for whether FEMA should recommend estimating an FPF.

Data on Costs of Labor

The Quarterly Census of Employment and Wages is a monthly census of employers, relying primarily on state unemployment insurance program data (through the quarterly contribution report[1]). The employer provides data on the number of establishments, the number of wage and salary workers, total and average wages for a specific time period, and the size of establishments within a geographical area. Data are aggregated to the county-quarter level (or the county-month level, in the case of monthly employment) for all industries (both public and private) that meet disclosure requirements.

Quarterly Census of Employment and Wages data are available at the county, metro area, state, and national geographies and at monthly, quarterly, and annual levels (depending on the variable—e.g., employment is the only variable available at a monthly level). See the Bureau of Labor Statistics' *Handbook of Methods* (U.S. Bureau of Labor Statistics, undated) for more detail.

Disaster-Specific Information

The Spatial Hazard Events and Losses Database for the United States (SHELDUS) is a longitudinal database compiling historical and current data on natural disasters, primarily from government sources. The database, originally developed by the University of South Carolina's Hazards and Vulnerability Research Institute and now maintained by Arizona State University's Center for Emergency Management and Homeland Security, measures aspects of natural disasters, such as event duration and human and monetary losses, across a variety of metrics (e.g., fatalities, property damage). The completeness and accuracy of these data make them an excellent source for research.

The aggregated version of the SHELDUS data, measured at the county level, compiles data from the following government sources:

- the National Centers for Environmental Information (made up of the former National Climatic Data Center and former National Geophysical Data Center)
- the U.S. Geological Survey
- the U.S. Department of Agriculture
- the National Aeronautics and Space Administration
- the Oregon Department of Geology and Mineral Industries
- FEMA's preliminary damage assessments

---

[1] The quarterly contribution report is supplemented by two additional surveys: the annual refiling survey and the multiple-worksite report. These surveys are meant to account for firms with multiple establishments or that span multiple industries, in that firm-level data submitted by firms in these cases are insufficiently disaggregated (see U.S. Bureau of Labor Statistics, 2021, p. 10).

- the U.S. Bureau of Labor Statistics
- the U.S. Census Bureau.

In addition, SHELDUS compiles data from academic publications and media reports. Some of the specific databases that are incorporated into SHELDUS include the following:

- the Significant Earthquake Database
- the Global Historical Tsunami Database
- the Significant Volcanic Eruptions Database
- Storm Data and Unusual Weather Phenomena.

The aggregated data represent sums of all outcomes (e.g., fatalities, property damage, crop damage) across individual events, by hazard type. The event-level data are also summed within counties and the month (or quarter) during which the events occurred. In the data for 1990 through 2018 are 16,763 county-disasters for which there is information on monetary value of economic losses.

The SHELDUS data are updated annually during November. For more detail, see the metadata page (Center for Emergency Management and Homeland Management, undated) on the SHELDUS website.

County-Level Information

We used two main data sources to get information on counties, which we used as covariates: the American Community Survey (ACS) and Statistics of Income. The ACS is an annual, national survey of 3.54 million addresses per year in the United States and Puerto Rico (U.S. Census Bureau, 2014). Specifically, the ACS surveys housing units (i.e., typical address) and group quarter facilities (e.g., college residence halls, residential treatment centers, skilled-nursing facilities, group homes, military barracks, correctional facilities, workers' dormitories, and facilities for homeless people) (U.S. Census Bureau, 2014). The purpose of the survey is to provide current and nationally consistent data to determine how to allocate more than $675 billion in federal and state funds every year. Statistics of Income migration data are produced by the Internal Revenue Service (IRS). These data use address changes from individual income tax returns to measure year-to-year migration patterns in the United States and are available for filing years 1991 through 2018. We used these data to measure the average per capita in-migration rates in each county, focusing only on households who migrate into a county from a different state. *In-migration* is defined as the number of tax filers moving into the county from out of state per 100 people already living in the county. Because the expert workshops suggested that labor supply issues could affect costs, we explored how the intensity with which workers were willing to move to an area before a disaster (the predisaster in-migration rate) might be correlated with costs. For more information on the data, see IRS, 2021.

CHAPTER THREE

Methodological Details

In this chapter, we describe our methods and approach. For the main building block of our analysis, we started by calculating a moving average of the change in construction wages, in percentage terms. Formally, we used this formula to calculate the percentage change in the average construction wage in county i for the T years after year t from what it was in the P years prior to the disaster:

$$\Delta y_{i,t} = \frac{\frac{1}{T}\sum_{k=1}^{T} y_{i,t+k} - \frac{1}{P}\sum_{k=1}^{P} y_{i,t-k}}{\frac{1}{P}\sum_{k=1}^{P} y_{i,t-k}},$$

where $\Delta y_{i,t}$ is the percentage change in the average construction wage in county i averaged over the T years after the disaster occurred (during year t) from what it was P years prior to the disaster.

Note that we excluded year t wages from the equation (i.e., $y_{i,t}$ does not actually enter this equation for $\Delta y_{i,t}$). This ensured that we did not need to adjust for when in the year the disaster hits the county. Also, we aimed to predict the change in wages averaged over the T years after the disaster because most of the PA expenditures do not occur immediately after the disaster. Choosing the number of periods to include involves a trade-off: A higher T potentially increases wage variability unrelated to the disaster in the estimate while also being a better reflection of the construction wages when the PA expenditures occurred. In our analysis, we assessed the average *real* (i.e., inflation-adjusted) wages during the five years after the disaster (i.e., $T = 5$). We chose $T = 5$ because our analysis suggests that, on average, approximately 10 to 15 percent of all PA expenditures occur in each of the first five years following a disaster, at which point the per-year expenditures begin to slow down (U.S. Government Accountability Office, 2008). Finally, we used $P = 2$ years before the disaster, instead of one year before, as a way to smooth out idiosyncratic shocks in the immediately predisaster year, $t - 1$.

Given these calculations of $\Delta y_{i,t}$, we plotted the distribution of wage changes in county-years following disasters and wage distribution in counties that did not encounter disasters (see Figure 3.1). Although the distribution of wage changes postdisaster (in solid blue) appears slightly to the right of the distribution of wage changes in counties without disasters (in dashed orange), the two distributions appear quite similar. This stems from the fact that

FIGURE 3.1

Distribution of $\Delta y_{i,t}$ in County-Years Where a Disaster Struck, as Changes

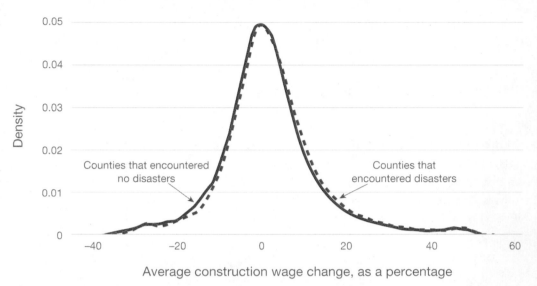

NOTE: The two lines represent the estimated kernel densities of the average construction wage changes.

the plots show the distribution of wage *changes*, not the distribution of *effects*. In other words, the $\Delta y_{i,t}$ measures combine both the effect of the disaster, which is what the FPF is designed to capture, and all the other idiosyncratic factors that can cause construction wages to change (e.g., standard pay increases). Note also that some of these other idiosyncratic factors might already be part of the part A or part B–H factors (i.e., the multipliers that can be applied to the part A estimate to adjust for factors influencing costs, as previously discussed) captured in a cost estimate, or something worth FEMA exploring as another factor. This is an important point. We needed to study the conditions or criteria for which a disaster-recovery effort was likely to *cause* large price increases because that is what an FPF value captures. An FPF is not a value capturing changes that might have occurred. Indeed, part A explicitly allows for disaster-related changes in unit costs, such as business-as-usual pay. By focusing on the effect of a disaster, this report can help reduce the risk of FEMA not estimating an FPF when it should and estimating an FPF when doing so is unnecessary. Our aim was therefore to estimate the distribution of effects, rather than the distribution of wage changes, because that is what an FPF is meant to capture.

Estimating the distribution of *effects* is more challenging than estimating the distribution of changes because effects are not directly observed. Data are collected on actual wages paid in a month. We can observe the average wages in the month before and after a disaster occurs. If wages increased after a disaster, we could not know whether the change observed was caused by the disaster, would have been that amount absent the disaster, or was the result of some combination of disaster-induced effects and general price changes. We needed some way of conducting analysis on the wage effects rather than the wage changes observed in the data. This is because, as discussed earlier, the criteria need to signal whether a location experiencing a disaster would likely experience large effects on prices because of that disaster.

To estimate the distribution of disaster effects, we developed a novel method that uses information from the areas over time not affected by disaster to determine what the distribution shown in orange in the figure would be if the true effect of the disasters were 0. If the only difference between the areas used for the curves in orange and blue is whether a disaster occurred, any differences between the two distributions could be attributed to the disaster. However, in reality, the areas represent different county-years with different characteristics, which, in turn, might differentially affect wage changes. Our approach accounts not only for the county-year characteristics but also for the fact that wage changes are inherently noisy. To determine the effect distribution, we could then compare the simulated distribution to the observed distribution. We next discuss the approach in more detail, with a particular focus on the assumptions it uses to identify the effect distribution.

The Estimation Approach

We propose a maximum-likelihood deconvolution with Bayesian inference approach to estimate the effect of a disaster on construction wages. We start by noting that the average percentage change between pre- and postdisaster wages, $\Delta y_{i,t}$, can, in theory, be decomposed into two components: the effect of the disaster on wages and everything else that leads to wage changes. We write this as

$$\Delta y_{i,t} = \tau_{i,t} + \epsilon_{i,t},$$

where $\tau_{i,t}$ is the disaster's effect on construction wage changes and $\epsilon_{i,t}$ is the effect of everything else (i.e., the error term). Notice that $\tau_{i,t}$ is specific to county i and year t, which is consistent with our interest in the distribution of county-level effects rather than in some average value of $\tau_{i,t}$, which is the outcome studied in the past research cited above.

Cases in which the true signal (here, $\tau_{i,t}$) is observed only with noise (i.e., $\epsilon_{i,t}$) are well studied in several scientific disciplines, and much work has attempted to study how to "deconvolve" the signal from the noise when the distribution of the noise is known (see Bonhomme and Robin, 2010, for an example of wage deconvolution using the Panel Study of Income Dynamics). In the context of causal inference, unlike in signal processing, the distribution of the error term is not known. Any observations that are not treated (in this case, exposed to a disaster) are control observations. Fortunately, there are some control observations—in our case, county-year observations—that were not affected by disasters. Our approach was to use these control observations to help identify the distribution of the error term and then apply existing deconvolution approaches to identify the distribution of the $\tau_{i,t}$ effects. In addition to relaxing the assumption of an a priori known error distribution, our approach does not assume that county-year error terms are identically distributed, as is common in the deconvolution literature, but allows county differences in the mean and standard deviation of the error distribution. Specifically, the mean (β) and standard deviation (δ) are allowed to vary by county such that they are captured by linear functions of observed, county-level characteristics, $\beta X_{i,t} - 1$ and $\delta X_{i,t} - 1$, as defined below.

These control observations are helpful because we know that the disaster effect, $\tau_{i,t}$, is equal to 0 for all of these observations because they did not experience disasters. Therefore, we can use them to understand the distribution of $\epsilon_{i,t}$. There are multiple ways to do this; we assumed that

$$\epsilon_{i,t} \sim N\left(\beta X_{i,t-1}, \delta X_{i,t-1}\right),$$

where β and δ are parameters that can be estimated from existing data. We assume that the error terms are normally distributed with mean equal to some linear function of $X_{i,t-1}$ and the variance also equal to a (different) linear function of $X_{i,t-1}$, where the Xs are covariates measuring attributes of the county i at time $t - 1$. Further research could consider the implication of assuming another distribution, such as a generalized extreme-value distribution (e.g., Gumbel), to capture that damage estimates determine what is a disaster and that therefore this is likely to be a distribution of maxima.

As covariates, each represented by X, we included the inverse population size of the county, the number of people per capita who moved into the county from a different state (in-migration), the unemployment rate, the poverty rate, the ratio of construction wages in the county to construction wages in the United States, and the ratio of rent in the county to average rent in the United States. To ensure that the measures are exogenous and observable at the time of the disaster (and can, therefore, be used by FEMA in determining whether estimating an FPF is warranted), all are measured with a lag, which is why the covariate vector is written as $X_{i,t-1}$. These covariates are the same covariates we explored as potential correlates of the disaster cost effects, as described in Chapter Five, and were chosen based on findings of the expert workshops conducted as part of this project. Finally, it is worth noting that including the covariates in this way limits the dynamics of construction wage changes in a county by assuming that we need to control for only the year $t - 1$ values of the covariates.

We do not observe $\epsilon_{i,t}$ separately from $\tau_{i,t}$ for the county-year observations when a disaster hits. By contrast, for the county-year observations in which a disaster did not hit, we know that $\tau_{i,t} = 0$ and that therefore $\Delta y_{i,t} = \epsilon_{i,t}$.[1] Thus, we could use the control observations to estimate β and δ by running two regressions, both using $X_{i,t}$ as the covariates: The first uses $\Delta y_{i,t}$ as an outcome to estimate β, and the second uses $\left(\Delta y_{i,t} - \hat{\beta} X_{i,t}\right)^2$ as an outcome to estimate δ.

---

[1] Note that we consider $\Delta y_{i,t}$ to be a control observation, even if a disaster hit in year $t + 2$, so a portion of the five-year average consists of time when the county was recovering from a disaster. Put another way, we assumed that the risk of encountering a future disaster is one of the many shocks that could affect the county and that the shocks were part of what generates the relatively large variance of $\epsilon_{i,t}$.

Next, we defined F as the cumulative distribution function of impacts $\tau_{i,t}$. Note that estimating this distribution F and using it to estimate the fraction of disasters that cause large increases in construction costs is one of the main goals of this procedure. Knowledge of F would allow us to answer the question of what fraction of disasters cause construction wages to increase by more than 10 percent. Given the estimates of $\hat{\beta}$ and $\hat{\delta}$, the log-likelihood of observing $\Delta y_{i,t}$ for some observation (i,t) affected by a storm, conditional on $\hat{\beta}S_{i,t}, \hat{\delta}X_{i,t}$, and F, can be written as[2]

$$\ell\left(\Delta y_{i,t} \mid \hat{\beta}X_{i,t}, \hat{\delta}X_{i,t}, F\right) = \log\left(\int\left[\phi\left(\frac{\Delta y_{i,t} - \hat{\beta}X_{i,t} - \tau}{\hat{\delta}X_{i,t}}\right)dF(\tau)\right]\right), \qquad (3.1)$$

where $\phi(.)$ is the normal probability density function.

If we were willing to assume that the observations were independently distributed, we could then write the overall likelihood of observing the sample (conditional on $\hat{\beta}X_{i,t}, \hat{\delta}X_{i,t}$, and F) as being

$$\mathcal{L} = \frac{1}{NT}\sum\log\left(\int\left[\phi\left(\frac{\Delta y_{i,t} - \hat{\beta}X_{i,t} - \tau}{\hat{\delta}X_{i,t}}\right)dF(\tau)\right]\right), \qquad (3.2)$$

That said, the observations are not necessarily independent. There is potentially both serial autocorrelation (i.e., correlation within counties across time periods) and spatial autocorrelation (i.e., correlation across counties within time periods) in the shocks to construction wages (i.e., in the $\epsilon_{i,t}$ terms). Furthermore, disasters also likely have both serial and spatial autocorrelation effects on construction wages (i.e., in the $\tau_{i,t}$ measures). Despite the clear correlations across observations, we still estimated F by maximizing a version of Equation 3.2. It is likely that, with some constraints on the autocorrelations, this would still be a consistent (if not efficient) estimate of F; see Wooldridge, 2010, on partial maximum likelihoods for more details. However, it was beyond the scope of this project to show this proof.

An additional difficulty in estimating F stems from the fact that Equation 3.1 suggests that we needed to optimize over an infinite dimensional cumulative distribution function. Although approaches to estimating such a function exist (e.g., Koenker and Mizera, 2014) and are reasonably well understood, the maximization is computationally challenging, and the results can be difficult to interpret. Instead, we estimated F by specifying a finite grid

---

[2] Note that conditioning on $\hat{\beta}X_{i,t}, \hat{\delta}X_{i,t}$, and F is slightly different from conditioning on $X_{i,t}$, in that conditioning on $X_{i,t}$ would mean conditioning on the conditional distribution of F given $X_{i,t}$ (i.e., on $\hat{\beta}X_{i,t}, \hat{\delta}X_{i,t}$, and $F \mid X_{i,t}$) rather than on the unconditional distribution of F. We ignore this subtle but potentially important issue in this discussion but return to the issue later.

and maximizing over this discrete distribution rather than the continuous distribution as in Equation 3.1 or 3.2. Specifically, we chose $\hat{F}$ such that

$$\hat{F} = \arg\max\left\{\frac{1}{NT}\sum\log\left[\sum_{k=1}^{1,000}\left[\phi\left(\frac{\Delta y_{i,t} - \hat{\beta}X_{i,t} - \tau_k}{\hat{\delta}X_{i,t}}\right)\Pr(\tau = \tau_k)\right]\right]\right\}. \quad (3.3)$$

We used an evenly spaced grid of τ_k values that spanned the range of observed values of $\Delta y_{i,t}$. Note that, because we used a discrete distribution, $\Pr(\tau = \tau_k)$ was just equal to the difference in the cumulative distribution function $F(\tau_k) - F(\tau_{k-1})$.

Implied Assumptions

Some assumptions are implied by our approach to choose $\hat{F}$ as defined in Equation 3.3. We now discuss these assumptions in more detail, focusing here on the economic nature of these assumptions rather than on the mathematical specification. We organized the set of assumptions into two groups: the assumptions needed for Equation 3.1 to be an accurate representation of the individual likelihood and the assumptions required to move from the individual likelihood in Equation 3.1 to Equation 3.3.

As discussed above, the main assumption needed for Equation 3.1 is that $\epsilon_{i,t} \sim N(\beta X_{i,t-1}, \delta X_{i,t-1})$, but what does that assumption imply? One of the important implications of this is an assumption that construction wages following county-years hit by a disaster would have evolved similarly to other county-years in the same $X_{i,t}$ and no disaster, had no disaster actually occurred. Put another way, this assumption amounts to assuming that the timing of when a county is hit by a disaster is more or less random. A second implication of the assumption that $\epsilon_{i,t} \sim N(\beta X_{i,t-1}, \delta X_{i,t-1})$ is that the distribution of wage changes is normal, after accounting for $X_{i,t}$.

The second set of assumptions involved allowing us to use Equation 3.3 as a way to estimate $\hat{F}$, given that the individual likelihood in Equation 3.1 is the correct likelihood. As discussed above, these assumptions are more technical in nature. One component of this assumption is that there is a unique maximum of Equation 3.3. Although theoretical results suggest that this is the case (e.g., Kiefer and Wolfowitz, 1956), from a practical perspective, there could be many functions that almost maximize Equation 3.3, and that fact leads to uncertainty in the true maximum. In Appendix A, we report on our simulations to explore how well identified Equation 3.3 is under various treatment effect distributions. We found that the approach does relatively well at identifying the true-effect distribution, even given the limited sample size, although identifying sharp changes in the underlying distribution is challenging. Most notably, we found that, in a right-skewed distribution with strictly positive values, we could identify the right skew, but the resulting distribution incorrectly suggests that some of the values of the underlying distribution are negative.

Computational Considerations

Although it is not infinitely dimensional, maximizing Equation 3.3 is still challenging given the high numbers of parameters and constraints. We use a grid size of 1,000, which means that 1,000 parameters were involved in the maximization and 1,001 constraints; 1,000 of the constraints are that each parameter must be weakly positive, with the additional constraint being that the parameters must sum to 1. Instead of directly maximizing Equation 3.3, we used an iterative algorithm that is a simplified version of an expectation–maximization algorithm, which is known to converge to the local maximum in this context (Laird, 1978).

In the algorithm, we first assumed a distribution F_0; by definition, this gives an estimate of $\Pr_0\left(\tau = \tau_k\right)$ for each grid point τ_k. Given the assumption of a normally distributed error term, we knew that

$$\Pr\left(\Delta y_{i,t} \mid \tau_k, \hat{\beta} X_{i,t-1}, \hat{\delta} X_{i,t-1}\right) = \phi\left(\frac{\Delta y_{i,t} - \hat{\beta} X_{i,t-1} - \tau_k}{\hat{\delta} X_{i,t-1}}\right).$$

Given these two formulas, we could use Bayes's law to determine the probability that an observation lies in each of the τ_k bins. This formula gave us

$$\Pr_0\left(\tau = \tau_k \mid \Delta y_{i,t}, \hat{\beta} X_{i,t-1}, \hat{\delta} X_{i,t-1}\right) = \frac{\Pr\left(\Delta y_{i,t} \mid \tau_k, \hat{\beta} X_{i,t-1}, \hat{\delta} X_{i,t-1}\right) \Pr_0\left(\tau = \tau_k\right)}{\Pr\left(\Delta y_{i,t}\right)}.$$

Because we knew that

$$\sum_{\forall \tau_k} \Pr\left(\tau = \tau_k \mid \Delta y_{i,t}, \hat{\beta} X_{i,t-1}, \hat{\delta} X_{i,t-1}\right) = 1,$$

we could generate estimates of $\Pr_0\left(\tau = \tau_k \mid \Delta y_{i,t}, \hat{\beta} X_{i,t-1}, \hat{\delta} X_{i,t-1}\right)$ for each county i and year t observation.

Doing so for all observations, we could then generate another distribution F_1 by adding up the probabilities for each observation and dividing by the total number of counties N and years T ($N * T$) to estimate an expected value of the probability:

$$\Pr_1\left(\tau = \tau_k\right) = \frac{1}{NT} \sum \Pr_0\left(\tau = \tau_k \mid \Delta y_{i,t}, \hat{\beta} X_{i,t-1}, \hat{\delta} X_{i,t-1}\right).$$

Similarly, we could use this estimated distribution F_1 and Bayes's law to determine the probability that an observation lies in each of the bins, add up the probability for each bin over all observations, and obtain a third distribution F_2. Note that the only reason that F_2 will differ from F_1 is that F_1 was estimated using F_0 as the prior and F_2 was estimated using F_1 as the prior. Existing results (Feng and Dicker, 2018) suggest that repeating this procedure to create a sequence of estimates $F_0, F_1, F_2, F_3, F_4 \ldots F_N$ will result in distributions that converge to the distribution that maximizes Equation 3.3. In practice, we repeated the procedure K times, until $\left\| F_K - F_{K-1} \right\| < 10^{-5}$, where we measured the distance between two discrete distributions as the sum of the squared differences in probabilities for each of the bins. The estimation was done in Python.

CHAPTER FOUR

Results of the Cost Effects of Disasters

We now present the results of the analysis. We began by looking across all disasters that caused property damage in excess of $10 per person in an affected county and estimated the distribution of effects that these disasters have had on average construction wages. We then used this underlying distribution and the observed changes in costs to estimate which disasters caused the largest increases in average construction costs using an empirical Bayes's method. Recall that we focused on the *causal* effect of a disaster, rather than changes, because FEMA already used B–H factors in the CEF to account for other cost changes. Therefore, we "removed" the change in costs that might have occurred anyway in the absence of a disaster that an FPF was not designed to capture. The FPF was designed to capture cost increases due to economic effects of a disaster. That said, it might be important for FEMA to consider whether this piece "removed" is indeed included somewhere in part B–H factors.

How Many Disasters Caused Wage Increases of More Than 10 Percent?

Figure 4.1 shows the estimated distribution of $\tau_{i,t}$ values (i.e., the distribution of *impacts* on construction wages in a county after a disaster hits) as the solid blue line. When we contrast this with the raw wage change (the dashed orange line), which shows the distribution of wage *changes* after a disaster, it is immediately clear that Figure 4.1 vastly overstates the proportion of disasters that caused an increase in construction wages of at least 10 percent. Although wage changes of greater than 20 percent or less than –20 percent were relatively common, the estimated distribution of effects suggests that most of these changes were due to factors other than the disaster itself.

Notably, the effect distribution illustrated in Figure 4.1 does have a right tail, suggesting that some disasters do cause large increases in construction wages. We found that approximately 4 percent of postdisaster counties had effects of more than 10 percent. Our findings imply that measuring changes (rather than effects) greatly overstates the need for FPFs, such that estimating an FPF would be warranted in only approximately 4 percent of postdisaster counties. It is reassuring to note that the left tail (i.e., decreases in wages) is much lower in the effect distribution than in the change distribution. Although the random variation in wages can result in wage decreases, we estimated that disasters caused decreases in average con-

FIGURE 4.1

Distribution of $\Delta y_{i,t}$ in County-Years Where a Disaster Struck: Effects and Changes

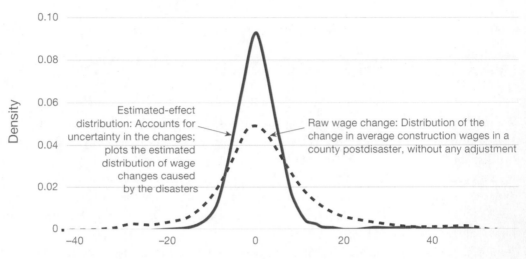

Average construction wage change, as a percentage

struction wages of 10 percent or more in less than 1 percent of counties and that virtually no county saw a decrease in average wages of 20 percent or more due to a disaster.

This skew in the distribution highlights the importance of estimating the distribution non-parametrically. From the perspective of this research, it also suggests that some disasters—albeit few—do require FPFs.

Do Compositional Changes Complicate the Analysis?

A disaster could cause the average construction wages to decrease if it changes the makeup of the construction workforce. For example, suppose that a rebuild requires a relatively large number of unskilled construction laborers (paid below-average construction wages) and relatively few electricians (who are paid above-average construction wages); in this case, average construction wages might fall even if the wages of both electricians and unskilled construction laborers were to increase postdisaster.

Although we could not completely rule out this explanation, our data allowed us to estimate the effect of disasters on more-detailed measures of the construction workforce, such as those broken down by three-digit North American Industry Classification System codes. These allowed us to separately estimate the effects on three subcategories of construction work: construction of buildings, heavy and civil engineering construction, and specialty trade contractors. The estimated-effect distributions for the three sectors are similar, suggesting that compositional changes across sectors were not responsible for the estimated effect on average construction wages. Further analysis using Standard Occupational Classification codes within construction industries could also be performed to determine whether disasters affect the composition of occupations within industries.

An alternative approach would be to directly control for skill composition and other observables when computing the mean and variance of the effect distribution. Doing so, however, would come at the cost of specifying a parametric form for the effect distribution, so compositional changes would be assumed to affect the entire shape of the distribution in a similar way. Because our focus in this project was explicitly on the right tail of the effect distribution, we opted for the nonparametric approach to flexibly estimate the right tail.

CHAPTER FIVE

Potential Criteria: Correlates of Disaster Cost Effects

In Chapter Four, we showed that about 4 percent of counties hit by disaster see increases in average construction wages of at least 10 percent in the five years postdisaster. We next explored how characteristics of the county and disaster affect the likelihood of that happening, starting with the size of the disaster and then moving toward characteristics about the county. Note that our goal in this section was not to understand the mechanisms behind the large increases or to inform FEMA about potential ways to reduce the cost of a rebuild. Instead, we aimed to predict which characteristics were correlated with the large increases. These predictions will become criteria to guide FEMA policy about when it should ask for an FPF estimate. Importantly, as we discuss later, these recommendations are only the first stage in a two-stage model. If the estimated FPF does not yield results that indicate a 10-percent increase or more in costs, estimating an FPF is not warranted. From a practical perspective, this first stage means that we explored each of the county characteristics individually and did not simultaneously control for the other characteristics.

Estimating the correlates of wage effects was challenging because, as before, we were less concerned with understanding how characteristics altered the average effect than with how they altered the probability of a large wage effect. After settling on the covariate of interest, we therefore repeated the estimation procedure as defined by Equation 3.3 in Chapter Three, restricting the sample to include only counties in which the value of the covariate of interest was near a fixed point of the covariate distribution. We then repeated this process at multiple fixed points to generate an estimate of the probability of wage-change effect values at multiple points on the covariate distribution. We then fit a line through these resulting points using a local polynomial regression to map how the probability (of a disaster causing the average construction wages in a county to increase by more than 10 percent) depended on the log per capita property damage.

Stated differently, this step involves, in this order,

1. iteratively estimating the posterior distribution at multiple points on the covariate distribution
2. calculating quantiles of these posterior distributions

3. fitting local polynomial regressions through those quantile estimates to understand the relationship between the covariate and the treatment effect quantiles.

This method is therefore essentially the same as running a kernel regression with a uniform kernel, although, instead of estimating $\mathbb{E}\left[\tau \mid X_{i,t}\right]$ using a local regression, we estimated $\Pr\left(\tau > 10 \mid X_{i,t}\right)$ using the method defined above. Better understanding the optimal bandwidth of this result and the statistical properties, such as the confidence intervals, is interesting but beyond the scope of this project.

The Relationship Between Disaster Size and Construction Wage Changes

We first explored the most natural characteristic: disaster size. Although we explored different ways to measure disaster size, we settled on measuring disaster size as the per capita property damage experienced in a county due to a disaster, as reported in SHELDUS. We settled on this metric for two main reasons. First, relying on property damage rather than physical characteristics of a disaster, such as wind speed, rainfall, or acres burned, allowed us to include multiple types of disasters in our analysis. Second, we used estimated property damage as opposed to PA expenditures in large part because the property damage estimates are usually made by the National Oceanic and Atmospheric Administration in the immediate aftermath of a disaster and therefore available to all parties quickly after a disaster; as of this writing in November 2020, for example, data through August 2020 were available. Other metrics, such as property damage values available via preliminary damage assessments, are not available in a timely manner for large disasters that typically go through an expedited process without damage assessments completed (FEMA, 2020b).

The results, shown in in Figure 5.1, are stark. Disasters causing less than $1,000 per capita in property damage almost never raised average construction wages by more than 10 percent. That is, the probability of increasing wages by 10 percent or more is nearly 0. Even a disaster that causes $1,000 in property damage per person in the county has less than a 5-percent chance of increasing average construction wages by more than 10 percent. The probability that a disaster will cause significant increases in average construction wage begins to increase after the $1,000 per capita threshold. For example, about one in five county-disasters that cause $10,000 per person in property damage increases average construction wages by more than 10 percent. In short, disaster size appears to be a necessary, but not sufficient, condition for a disaster to increase construction wages by more than 10 percent.

FIGURE 5.1

The Relationship Between Per Capita Property Damage and the Probability of a Cost Increase of at Least 10 Percent

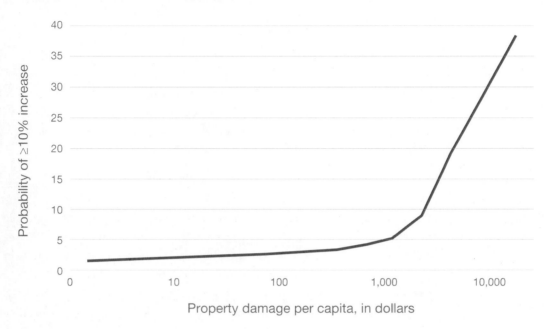

The Relationship Between Disaster Size, In-Migration, and Construction Wage Changes

We next explored county characteristics affecting the probability that a disaster will increase average construction wages by more than 10 percent. Given the previous result that only large disasters cause increases in average construction wages, we illustrated the results by first dividing the counties hit by disasters into three strata based on property damage. Then, we redid the analysis of property damage per capita for each of the three strata of counties. This ensured that we did not mistakenly search for county characteristics that were correlated with disaster size. It also provided a robustness check to ensure that the county characteristics increased the effect that a disaster has on average construction wage changes rather than merely being correlated with average construction wage changes, disaster or no disaster. If a county's stratum is predictive of large construction wage changes across all disaster sizes, it is likely that this is not due to mediating the effect of a disaster.[1]

---

[1] In an ordinary-least-squares regression, this is equivalent to the difference between the coefficient on a covariate and a coefficient on a covariate interacted with the treatment. In our method, the baseline correlation is controlled for via $\hat{\beta}$, but a nonlinear relationship between the covariate and outcome or uncertainty in the coefficient estimates could mean that this is insufficient.

Finally, we note that the county characteristics we explored came from our expert workshops. To inform which variables to study as potential correlates, we conducted workshops about hypothetical future disasters (or scenarios) and elicited a range of variables to test as potential correlates.

Even with a wide variety of scenario locations and disaster types throughout the United States, all workshop discussions focused on understanding how and when the number of workers needed for a recovery in a county could easily increase during a rebuild without requiring excess wage increases (or, in economic terms, whether the supply of labor, usually construction labor, in the county is elastic). Given this, in this chapter, we provide results on correlations with metrics for "isolation" or "attractiveness" and latent workforce; other characteristics tested and shown not to be correlated are presented in Appendix B.

A County's Isolation

In our first stratification, we split counties into three groups depending on how often people migrate from other states into the county. The groups were chosen so that roughly one-quarter of the sample was in the low–in-migration bin, half was in the medium–in-migration bin, and the remaining quarter was in the high–in-migration bin.

As can be seen in Figure 5.2, it appears that a county's isolation, when measured this way, is quite predictive of whether average construction wages will increase postdisaster. Counties that had historically low in-migration were quite likely to see increases in their average construction wages after large disasters; in contrast, we found that areas with high in-migration rates never saw large increases, even after large disasters. Note that, in this analysis, in-migration was measured in the year predisaster.

An alternative measure of a county's isolation is its rural designation, as defined by the U.S. Department of Agriculture (Figure 5.3). It tells a similar story, in that rural counties were the most likely to see an increase in average construction wages after large disasters, as indicated by the vertical distance between the rural line and the other lines. Although a metro or metro-adjacent county is less likely to see an increase in average construction wages after disasters of most sizes, a metro county has a higher probability of seeing a large increase after the largest disasters. This stratification thus does not explain as much of the difference in the probability of a large average wage increase as a county's in-migration rate does; the county's in-migration rate shows a clear vertical ordering as disaster size increases.

A County's Latent Construction Workforce

Another way of increasing the size of the construction workforce is to have people already in the county enter construction occupations either from other occupations or from unemployment. Researchers have previously calculated the probability that someone will move into the construction industry from a different occupation (Gonzalez et al., 2020). We used these probabilities to calculate the size of a county's latent construction workforce by weighting the proportion of people working in each occupation in the county in the year before the disaster

FIGURE 5.2

The Relationship Between Per Capita Property Damage and the Probability of a Cost Increase of at Least 10 Percent, by In-Migration Rate

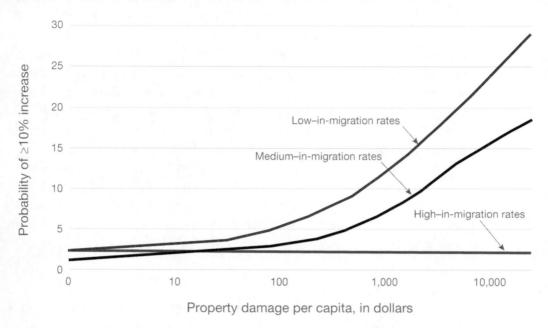

FIGURE 5.3

The Relationship Between Per Capita Property Damage and the Probability of a Cost Increase of at Least 10 Percent, by Rural Designation

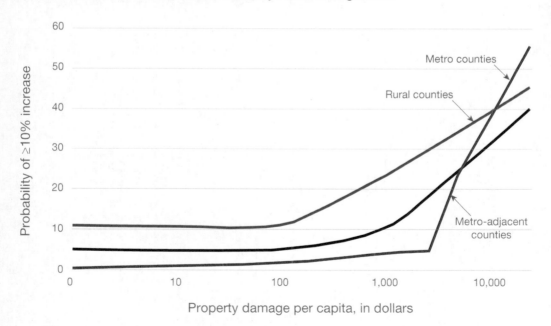

by the probability that people in those occupations will switch to construction jobs. In addition, we determined the county's baseline unemployment rate. We recognize, however, that this is not something that FEMA would be able to do after each disaster. We provide this information to begin to understand whether the in-migration rate is picking up on the available labor force, as was discussed in expert workshops as well.

These results are shown in Figure 5.4 and Figure 5.5. The results suggest that a county with a medium rate of unemployment in the baseline period has a larger probability of seeing large average construction wage increases postdisaster than counties with either low or high unemployment rates. This is a bit perplexing, in that we would expect wages to be most sensitive to a disaster in areas with low unemployment. One possibility is that there is an omitted-variable bias, a variable correlated with both unemployment and wage effects, that complicates the analysis. We also cannot rule out that the results were due to uncertainty inherent in the estimates. In contrast, the story is more consistent with classical economic theory when analyzing the size of the latent construction workforce using people from other occupations. Although these results are relatively noisy, it does appear that the larger this latent workforce is, the less likely it is that a disaster will cause large average construction wage changes in the county.

FIGURE 5.4

The Relationship Between Per Capita Property Damage and the Probability of a Cost Increase of at Least 10 Percent, by Unemployment Level

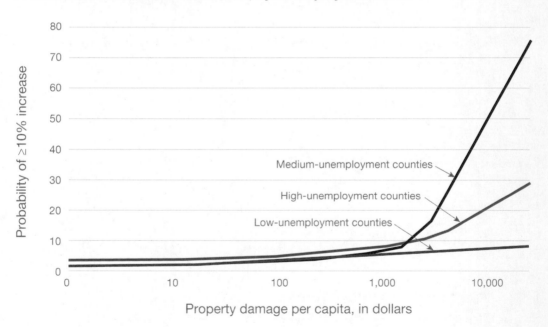

FIGURE 5.5

The Relationship Between Per Capita Property Damage and the Probability of a Cost Increase of at Least 10 Percent, by the Size of the Latent Construction Workforce

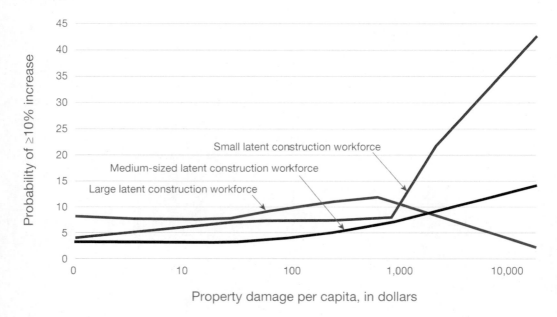

CHAPTER SIX

Assessing Potential Thresholds

A FEMA cost estimator must determine whether criterion thresholds are met and therefore an FPF would be applied. We now explore potential thresholds for per capita property damage and in-migration. We considered the proportion of county-disasters estimated to have small (less than 10 percent) or large (10 percent or greater) average construction wage effects based on different thresholds for the criteria of property damage per capita and in-migration.

When setting recommended thresholds, there is a tension between false positives (e.g., overpredicting the number of disasters that cause large increases in average wages) and false negatives (e.g., missing disasters that do cause large increases in average wages). The question is whether there are thresholds past which most of the disasters that cause an increase of more than 10 percent are correctly predicted (true positive) and most of the disasters that do not cause an increase of more than 10 percent are correctly predicted as not having large increases (true negative), all while keeping the false-positive and false-negative rates low. Setting a low criterion would allow us to correctly identify all disasters with large wage increases; however, it would also lead to failure to identify disasters that actually had small wage increases. Setting a criterion too low would mean lots of false positives because, our results suggest, these large increases rarely occur. For more about how we generated the thresholds, see Appendix C.

It is important to note that calculating this trade-off for this study was challenging. We cannot know for certain which county-disasters actually experienced construction wage effects of certain amounts. These are estimated. We can only estimate whether a disaster will cause an increase of more than 10 percent and cannot observe that directly. Therefore, we provide information on "FPF-warranted matches" (as true positives) and "no FPF–warranted matches" (as true negatives).

Potential Thresholds

We considered six possible thresholds, listed in Table 6.1. In each row of the table, we list one threshold for disaster size (e.g., at least $1,000 in damage per capita of a county) and one for the in-migration rate (e.g., less than 2.5-percent in-migration rate). The third column provides the fraction of all county-disasters that meet both criteria.

Generally speaking, the more stringent the thresholds, the fewer county-disasters meet the thresholds. At a threshold of at least $1,000 per capita in damage (criteria 1 and 2), approxi-

TABLE 6.1

Thresholds for Assessment

	Criterion Threshold		
Criterion	Disaster Size, in Dollars of Damage	In-Migration, as a Percentage	Percentage of County-Disasters in the Data Meeting This Criterion
1	>1,000	None	9.1
2		<2.5	4.9
3	>5,000	None	2.6
4		<2.5	1.3
5	>10,000	None	1.4
6		<2.5	0.8

mately 9.1 percent of county-disasters experienced disasters of this size. We examined thresholds through $10,000 per capita or more in damage (criteria 5 and 6), and approximately 2.6 and 1.4 percent, respectively, of county-disasters experienced disasters of this size. Note that, overall, we estimated that 4 percent of county-disasters had large wage effects, warranting estimation of an FPF. Therefore, it is likely that a threshold of $1,000 flags too many county-disasters and $10,000 does not flag enough disasters. This is suggestive that a disaster with less than $1,000 per capita in damage does not require an FPF and that damage levels of $1,000 to $10,000 per capita need more information or another criterion. We cannot be sure whether there is an amount greater than $10,000 at which every county-disaster should have an FPF estimate; we address this in Chapter Seven.

Threshold Assessment

We reviewed two metrics to assess these six criteria:

- *FPF-warranted match* (*true positive*) refers to the fraction of county-disasters with wage effects of 10 percent or more that match the criteria.
- *No FPF–warranted matches* (*true negative*) refers to the fraction of county-disasters that are unlikely to experience wage effects of 10 percent or more that match the criteria.

Figure 6.1 provides results of the assessment, with the bars indicating the proportion of FPF-warranted matches and the line referring to the proportion of no FPF–warranted matches. Generally speaking, we can see that, with each successive threshold, the FPF matches worsen and the no-FPF matches improve. Specifically, when adding the in-migration threshold of less than 2.5 percent, we found that 4.9 percent of county-disasters met criterion 2. This is approximately the proportion that we estimated likely had large price effects. Next we assessed what proportion of these 4.9 percent were "correctly" flagged as warranting FPF

FIGURE 6.1

Assessing Potential Thresholds

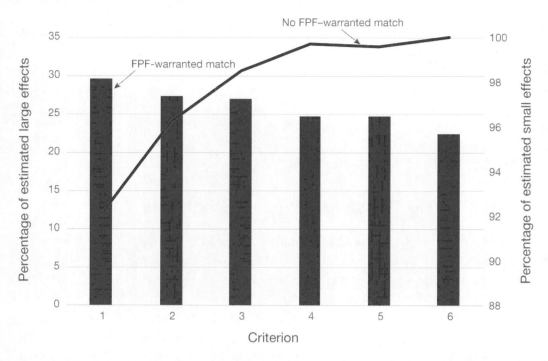

estimation. We found that 27.3 percent (of the 4.9 percent) were good matches, meaning that they were flagged as warranting FPFs when they were estimated to have large price effects due to disaster. We found that few (3.8 percent of the 4.9 percent) were poor matches as flagged warranting an FPF but unlikely to have large price effects. This criterion increasingly reduces the poor matches at damage thresholds of $5,000 (0.3 percent) and $10,000 (0.0 percent), although this is increasingly at the expense of missing some: We found decreasingly good match rates from 24.6 percent (criterion 4) to 22.4 percent (criterion 6). Therefore, the in-migration rate threshold of 2.5 percent is a useful additional criterion for disasters of $1,000 to $10,000 in damage per capita that limits the poor match rate while maintaining good match rates.

As summarized in Table 6.2, the thresholds we had assessed thus far suggest that disasters of less than $1,000 per capita in damage (in fiscal year [FY] 2018 dollars) are highly unlikely to cause large cost increases (those of 10 percent or greater), regardless of in-migration rate. Between $1,000 and $10,000 per capita, the in-migration rate matters, and areas with low in-migration rates are likelier to have large disaster effects. Beyond $10,000 per capita, an FPF is probably warranted, although the data contain very few disasters with this level of damage, so whether it is $10,000 per capita or another number is not yet well known.

TABLE 6.2

Preliminary Future Price Forecast Considerations Based on Threshold Assessment

Damage Per Capita, in FY 2018 Dollars	In-Migration Rate, as a Percentage	FPF Estimate Warranted
<1,000	Any	No
1,000+	<2.5	Yes
1,000–10,000	2.5+	Maybe[a]
10,000+	2.5+	Maybe[a]

[a] With few events in the data, stress testing would be needed.

Stress-Testing Thresholds: What-If Scenarios

We explored the implications of these criterion thresholds by estimating FPFs in some what-if scenarios using the same model (CGE) used for Puerto Rico and the USVI. Specifically, to better understand whether the model for an FPF would yield values of 1.10 or greater (indicating a disaster effect of 10 percent or more), we considered the impact of disasters with per capita damage of $1,000, $10,000, and greater than $10,000 in jurisdictions with low in-migration rates (less than 2.5 percent) and higher in-migration rates.

Because estimating an FPF is complex and labor-intensive, we could not estimate an FPF for every area in the United States. We necessarily needed to limit jurisdictions to a useful range of areas that

- did not meet either criterion (in terms of in-migration rates and per capita damage)
- met one criterion but not the other
- met both criteria.

This allowed us to explore the conditions under which the criterion thresholds perform well, or not, as indicators of a need to estimate an FPF. We considered cities, counties, metro areas, regions, and a state jurisdiction with a range of in-migration rates below and above the threshold of 2.5 percent. We also considered areas with a range of gross regional products (GRPs) from $300 million to $1.2 trillion (as an indication of the level of economic activity) and selected areas across the country at risk for a variety of natural disasters that typically cause large amounts of economic damage, including earthquakes, hurricanes, floods, and ice storms. This resulted in the selection of 16 jurisdictions mapped in Figure 6.2.

What-If Scenarios

First, we considered the threshold of $1,000 per capita in damage. We estimated FPFs for low– and high–in-migration jurisdictions; the methodology is described below and in detail in Appendix E. For each jurisdiction, we allowed for the range of PA spending paths over time

FIGURE 6.2
Gross Regional Products for What-If Scenario Jurisdictions

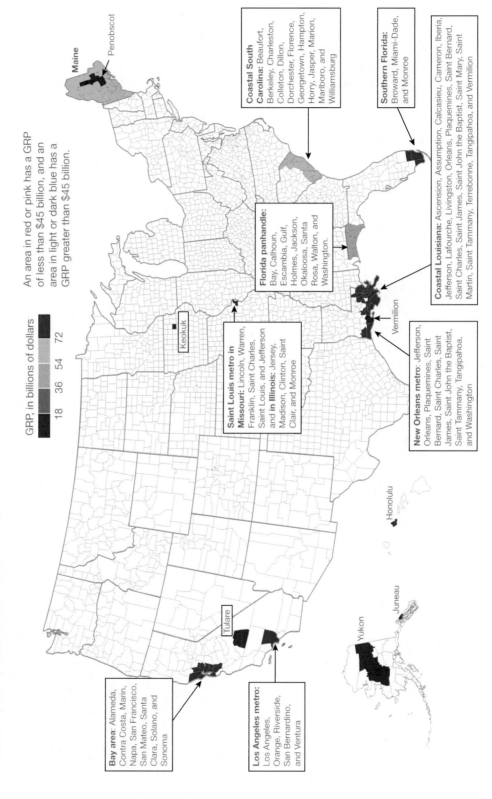

GRP, in billions of dollars

18   36   54   72

An area in red or pink has a GRP of less than $45 billion, and an area in light or dark blue has a GRP greater than $45 billion.

Maine

Penobscot

Coastal South Carolina: Beaufort, Berkeley, Charleston, Coleton, Dillon, Dorchester, Florence, Georgetown, Hampton, Horry, Jasper, Marion, Marlboro, and Williamsburg

Southern Florida: Broward, Miami-Dade, and Monroe

Florida panhandle: Bay, Calhoun, Escambia, Gulf, Holmes, Jackson, Okaloosa, Santa Rosa, Walton, and Washington.

Coastal Louisiana: Ascension, Assumption, Calcasieu, Cameron, Iberia, Jefferson, Lafourche, Livingston, Orleans, Plaquemines, Saint Bernard, Saint Charles, Saint James, Saint John the Baptist, Saint Mary, Saint Martin, Saint Tammany, Terrebonne, Tangipahoa, and Vermilion.

Vermilion

Keokuk

Saint Louis metro in Missouri: Lincoln, Warren, Franklin, Saint Charles, Saint Louis, and Jefferson and **in Illinois:** Jersey, Madison, Clinton, Saint Clair, and Monroe

New Orleans metro: Jefferson, Orleans, Plaquemines, Saint Bernard, Saint Charles, Saint James, Saint John the Baptist, Saint Tammany, Tangipahoa, and Washington

Honolulu

Tulare

Yukon

Juneau

Bay area: Alameda, Contra Costa, Marin, Napa, San Francisco, San Mateo, Santa Clara, Solano, and Sonoma

Los Angeles metro: Los Angeles, Orange, Riverside, San Bernardino, and Ventura

for a disaster recovery. With the findings described in Chapter Five, we anticipated that no jurisdiction would experience an effect on construction costs (i.e., every jurisdiction would yield an FPF estimate of 1.0 and therefore not warrant estimating an FPF).

Second, we considered the threshold of $10,000 per capita in damage. Again, we estimated an FPF for each low– and high–in-migration jurisdiction using a shock of $10,000 per capita in PA spending for a disaster recovery. In Chapter Five, we describe our finding that the probability of a large price effect is 30 percent for low–in-migration counties and 0 to 20 percent for medium– and high–in-migration counties, respectively. Therefore, we anticipated that three low–in-migration jurisdictions (30 percent of the 11 low–in-migration jurisdictions) would have FPFs of 1.10 or greater and that none of the five high–in-migration jurisdictions would have an FPF of 1.10 or greater.

Third, we considered much larger thresholds than assessed thus far. We considered two high-damage scenarios: Hurricane Maria ($50 billion in total damage) and Hurricane Katrina ($81 billion in total damage). We could not apply these levels of damage to all our jurisdictions because, in low-GRP areas, these damage amounts are unfeasibly high (e.g., 27,000 percent of GRP in Keokuk, Iowa). Instead, in low-GRP areas (any with a GRP of less than $45 billion), we considered one scenario of damage reaching 50 percent of GRP and another scenario of 100 percent of GRP. Obviously, we anticipated that a greater proportion of jurisdictions would have FPF estimates greater than 1.10 as the size of damage increased. We were interested to see whether

- there was an amount of damage per capita after which 100 percent of jurisdictions had FPF estimates of 1.10 or greater
- more low–in-migration than high–in-migration jurisdictions had FPF estimates of 1.10 or greater.

These scenarios gave us a variety of per capita damage–by–in-migration rates that we could use to better understand the relationship between the scale of a disaster, mobility into an area, and the impact on construction prices.

Methodology: Estimating a Future Price Forecast in Each Scenario

We estimated an FPF in each jurisdiction separately for each damage threshold (e.g., $1,000 per capita, $10,000 capita, $50 billion or 50 percent of GRP, $81 billion or 100 percent of GRP) and compared FPF estimates with potential criterion thresholds. To estimate an FPF, we adapted the original CGE model used to estimate an FPF in the Puerto Rico context with 2016 data to the continental U.S. context using 2018 data. For full details of the methodology, please see Appendix E.

Findings

In Figure 6.3, we show the findings from the what-if scenarios. We recommend not estimating an FPF if per capita damage is less than $1,000, and indeed the scenarios indicate that the probability of a project needing an FPF is close to 0 (FPF estimate = 1.0). We recommend estimating an FPF for any county-disaster with low in-migration and damage between $1,000 and $10,000 per capita, and the implication here is that few of these county-disasters will need FPFs (FPF greater than 1.10) applied to project cost estimates. Informed by the what-if scenarios, we also added the recommendation of estimating an FPF at $55,000 per capita in damage regardless of in-migration rate because results show that it is highly likely that every county experiencing a disaster this size will have an FPF greater than 1.10 in the CEF. From the what-if scenarios, we also learned that, for a county-disaster with between $10,000 and $55,000 in per capita damage and high in-migration, there is a chance that it needs an FPF. According to our knowledge of general equilibrium in economics, the likelihood of needing an FPF will be based on the county's composition of construction labor force and the price of labor, materials, and equipment in each of the PA categories (e.g., utilities).

Summary of the Threshold Assessment

We reviewed the proportion of county-disasters with estimates of large cost effects at different thresholds for disaster damage and in-migration rates to develop a preliminary set of recommendations. Then, we explored the implication of the recommendations using what-if

FIGURE 6.3

Summary of What-If Scenario Results, in Fiscal Year 2018 U.S. Dollars

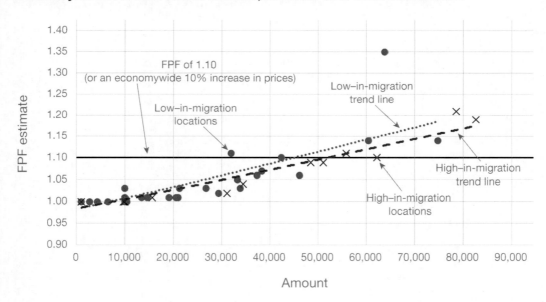

scenarios to estimate FPFs for a variety of jurisdictions and finalized those estimates based on our findings.

Our assessment suggests that there is still a great deal of uncertainty in predicting the economic impacts of disasters. Therefore, we recommend that receiving an FPF be a three-step process:

- In the first step, FEMA would determine whether the disaster meets predetermined thresholds to trigger the estimation of an FPF.
- If these trigger thresholds are met, FEMA would contract for an economic forecast for the region.
- If the forecast model anticipates future sustained costs in excess of 10 percent as a result of the disaster, the FPF factor would be adopted and used as part of the CEF.

This would provide FPF estimates only to those localities where it is warranted and would allow FEMA to adopt moderate standards to trigger the FPF calculation. Therefore, our recommendations are phrased as "FPF Estimate Warranted." Our findings and recommendations (all figures are in real 2018 dollars) are as shown in Table 6.3.

TABLE 6.3

Threshold Assessment Findings

Criterion		FPF Estimate Warranted		
County-Level Per Capita Damage, in FY 2018 U.S. Dollars	County In-Migration Rate, as a Percentage	Yes	No	Undetermined[a]
<1,000	Any		x	
1,000–10,000	<2.5	x		
	2.5+		x	
10,000–55,000	<2.5	x		
	2.5+			x
55,000+	Any	x		

[a] Indicates that analysis is needed to determine whether an FPF needs to be estimated.

CHAPTER SEVEN

Conclusions

We investigated the conditions under which a municipality or region would need an FPF in order to have sufficient funds to rebuild a community under a fixed-price contract, following what are known as alternative procedures. A fixed-price contract provides a lump-sum allotment to a regional government so that it can rebuild after a natural disaster. Because these fixed-price contracts cannot be renegotiated, both the local government and FEMA have a large incentive to estimate costs correctly. Unanticipated increases in costs can leave a community with too little money to rebuild. This is especially an issue when individual actors (contracting firms) do not consider the activities of all the other actors rebuilding in a community. If demand for inputs increases and contractors find themselves bidding up their prices in order to secure the inputs, it will be costlier to build a building after the disaster than it would have been before, and it would therefore be necessary to include an FPF in the fixed-price contract. In the vast majority of cases (more than 95 percent), the size and scope of a disaster does not warrant estimating an FPF (i.e., pressures on costs are modest). However, in a nontrivial proportion of disasters, the reconstruction effort itself affects market prices for labor, materials, and equipment, and an FPF might be warranted.

We needed to first identify when a locality experienced a 10-percent or greater increase in costs *caused* by the disaster because an FPF is one factor (of many in the CEF) that is supposed to capture economywide price increases due to the impact of a disaster and market frictions. We focused on labor costs—owing both to the availability of high-quality and timely data and to the fact that most of the demand-driven increase in prices of recovery projects is expected to be driven by labor costs. Motivated by expert scenario planning workshops, we tested a variety of community and disaster-related measures that might be predictive of large cost increases. We found strong support for the predictive power of two measures: disaster-related property damage per capita and in-migration.

Recommendations

This report provides guidance for FEMA to determine whether a locality should have an FPF estimated, as part of the standard cost estimation under fixed-price contracts (through alternative procedures), to adequately fund projects. Before we make recommendations on the criteria and thresholds to be used to trigger an FPF, we point out that, under ideal circumstances, application of an FPF is a three-step process:

- In the first step, FEMA determines whether the disaster meets predetermined thresholds to trigger the estimation of an FPF.
- If these trigger thresholds are met, then, in a second step, FEMA contracts for an economic forecast for the region.
- If the forecast model anticipates future sustained costs in excess of 10 percent as a result of the disaster, the FPF factor would be adopted and used as part of the CEF.

This three-step process has two advantages: First, it provides FPF estimates only to those localities where it is warranted. Second, it allows FEMA to adopt moderate standards to trigger the FPF calculation. By having more-moderate standards, FEMA minimizes the probability of making the costlier type II error (false negative)—*not* providing an FPF to a municipality when it actually needs one. The risk of a type I error (awarding an FPF to a locality that does not need one) is minimized by calculating an FPF and determining its value.

Any recommendation will come with uncertainty. Given the economic and social cost of failing to use an FPF when one might be necessary, combined with the evidence of this study (all figures are in real 2018 dollars), we propose the following recommendations:

- If PA damage is **less than $1,000** (in FY 2018 U.S. dollars), do not estimate an FPF.
- If PA damage is **between $1,000 and $10,000** per capita (in FY 2018 U.S. dollars) and
  - the in-migration rate is less than or equal to 2.5 percent, estimate an FPF.
  - the in-migration rate is greater than 2.5 percent, do not estimate an FPF.
- If PA damage is **between $10,000 and $55,000** per capita (in FY 2018 U.S. dollars) and
  - the in-migration rate is less than or equal to 2.5 percent, estimate an FPF.
  - the in-migration rate is greater than 2.5 percent, conduct a preliminary analysis to determine whether estimating an FPF is warranted.
- If PA damage is **$55,000 per capita or greater** (in FY 2018 U.S. dollars), estimate an FPF.

Disaster size in terms of property damage per capita is strongly predictive of when a community experiences construction wage increases in excess of 10 percent due to a disaster. Although there is no exact cutoff that predicts higher future costs with 100-percent accuracy, we recommend a lower bound of $1,000 per capita in damage. This number should be indexed to inflation using the same measure as CEF part E (i.e., either the Building Cost Index or the Construction Cost Index according to the *Engineering News-Record*).

For disasters leaving damage greater than $1,000 per capita but less than $55,000, we recommend combining the damage threshold with a measure of in-migration to the community. We recommend that, if average in-migration to a disaster-affected county is less than 2.5 percent (using Statistics of Income tax data [IRS, 2021]), FEMA commission economic research to estimate an FPF for the affected area. Data suggest that per capita damage estimates in the range of $1,000 to $55,000 (in FY 2018 U.S. dollars) combined with in-migration of 2.5 percent or less strikes a balance between false positives (which result in FEMA asking for an FPF estimate when further in-depth modeling indicates that one might not be necessary) and false negatives (which result in FEMA not asking for an FPF estimate, thereby underestimating the costs of reconstruction and failing to rebuild communities).

For disasters between $10,000 and $55,000 (in FY 2018 U.S. dollars) and high in-migration, two parts could be conducted in parallel with a preliminary analysis of the need for an FPF:

- The scale and composition of the construction labor force need to be determined. This can be accomplished using the most recent Occupational Employment and Wage Statistics from the Bureau of Labor Statistics. These data provide the number of workers in each of approximately 800 occupations and disaggregated to specific occupations, such as electrician, plumber, or construction laborer. Using preliminary damage estimates across all of the PA categories, occupational demand estimates can be obtained from input–output models relatively quickly. These demand estimates can then be combined with the supply estimates to consider how much the construction labor force would need to increase to incorporate the reconstruction effort. If either the scale or composition of the demand estimates is large relative to the supply, estimating an FPF curve might be warranted.
- The model used to estimate the FPF in Puerto Rico and the USVI, or an updated model, needs to be calibrated to the local conditions using IMPLAN data. Based on the preliminary damage estimates across PA categories, a preliminary FPF needs to be estimated. Because the model produces estimates of the price of labor, materials, and equipment in addition to the price of construction in each of the PA categories, if any of these prices yields an increase of greater than 10 percent, a formal FPF analysis would be recommended.

Our research shows that spending beyond $55,000 per capita (in FY 2018 U.S. dollars) leads to many market frictions and challenges in absorbing labor and capital that result in large price effects several years after a disaster. Very few disasters lead to this level of damage, so it would not be common and worth the trade-off.

An Important Consideration

We want to highlight the problem of the false negative (an area in need of an FPF that does not get one). Our recommendations provide a safety net for false positives in which FPF estimates are produced in areas where the criteria suggest that one is necessary and the estimate is either greater than 1.10 (and indeed the jurisdiction requires an FPF) or less than 1.10 (and the jurisdiction does not need one). However, thus far, our recommendations do not include a fail-safe for an area in which the criteria do not indicate estimation of an FPF but that, in the end, does require one.

We recommend that, to mitigate this risk, FEMA consider offering ex post corrections for jurisdictions that experience shocks. We recognize that current regulations do not permit price readjustments after agreement (FEMA, 2020c).[1] However, it is an uncertain world, and shocks can occur (e.g., catastrophic series of tornadoes); FEMA has noted this as well (FEMA, 2020a). These unanticipated shocks can lead to increased demand for labor and greater flows of spending than considered in the original cost estimate. This could lead to increased aggregate prices and leave jurisdictions unable to complete necessary projects within the initial cost estimate. Therefore, FEMA might need to consider whether, and when, an ex post correction to the decision of whether to estimate an FPF—perhaps not the entire cost estimate, but the decision to include an FPF—is needed in light of an unexpected event.

Implications of the Recommendations

How Often Might a Future Price Forecast Be Estimated?

According to IRS data on in-migration rates (78.5 percent of counties have in-migration rates of less than 2.5 percent) and SHELDUS data (8.9 percent of disasters leave more than $1,000 per capita in damage), approximately 7 percent of county-disasters have damage greater than $1,000 per capita and in-migration rates less than 2.5 percent. According to these two data sets again, few county-disasters (0.09 percent) meet the criteria of $10,000 to $55,000 per capita in damage (in FY 2018 U.S. dollars) and in-migration rates greater than 2.5 percent. Around 0.2 percent of county-disasters had more than $55,000 per capita in damage. Specifically, since 1990, nine disasters in 38 counties (not including Puerto Rico) have sustained damage of more than $55,000 per capita (in FY 2018 U.S. dollars). In other words, approximately one in every 500 county-disasters has damage of $55,000 per capita or greater (in FY 2018 U.S. dollars) and warrants an FPF estimation.

In sum, approximately seven in 100 county-disasters might be eligible to request estimation of an FPF using these criteria. With an average 600 county-disasters per year (per SHELDUS data), that is 42 county-disasters per year. It will likely be much lower than this number because an FPF is relevant only for projects using alternative procedures, which are currently utilized far less than standard procedures.

---

[1] The Office of Management and Budget establishes regulations regarding administrative requirements, cost principles, and audit requirements in 2 C.F.R. Part 200, Uniform Administrative Requirements, Cost Principles, and Audit Requirements for Federal Awards.

Where Is a Future Price Forecast Estimate More Likely to Be Warranted?

As shown in Figure 7.1, the 78.5 percent of counties (IRS, 2021) with in-migration rates less than 2.5 percent are not uniformly distributed across the country. Most counties of the Southwest, Pacific Northwest, and East Coast would not meet the criteria.

Disasters leaving damage of at least $55,000 per capita include hurricanes in the Gulf of Mexico between 1992 and 2018; a flood in Grand Forks, North Dakota, in 1997; a large fire in Los Alamos, New Mexico, in 2000; a series of tornado outbreaks in Kiowa County, Kansas, in 2007; a flood in Green County, Wisconsin, in 2008; and a flood in Tunica County, Mississippi, along the Mississippi River in 2011 (see Figure 7.2).

Areas of Potential Future Work

Although this report provides important insights into disasters' effects on costs, it is limited by a lack of extreme events in the data. There might be simply too few events to parse the data and predict all the reasons large price effects might occur. To supplement this study, we conducted a series of expert workshops to explore potential factors contributing to such

FIGURE 7.1
In-Migration Rates, by County

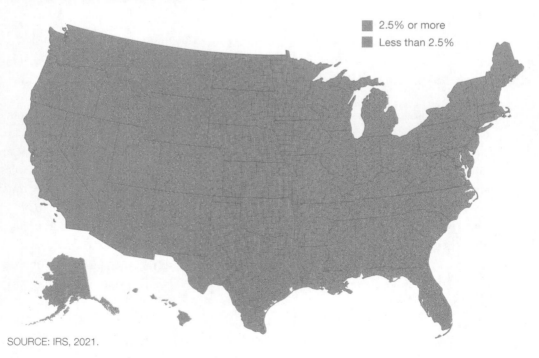

2.5% or more
Less than 2.5%

SOURCE: IRS, 2021.

FIGURE 7.2

Counties with Disaster Damage of at Least $55,000 Per Capita in Fiscal Year 2018 U.S. Dollars, 1960–2018

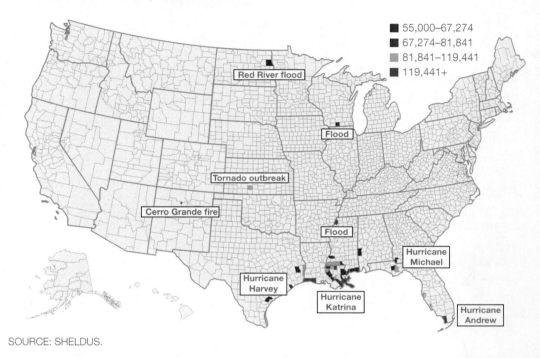

SOURCE: SHELDUS.

large price effects.[2] Discussions generated several hypotheses about the relationships between disasters and prices, some of which were tested in this study. Others, such as the following, were not within the scope of this project but are interesting avenues for further research:

- **predicting general wage changes:** One of the findings from the study is that, although few disasters cause large changes in average construction wages, average construction wages are not particularly stable over time, and increases of more than 20 percent are not uncommon. The wide distribution of wage changes, although they are not necessarily because of the disaster, suggests that there is a lot of uncertainty in how much contractors are going to have to pay, which likely decreases their willingness to bid on fixed-price contracts. In other words, as researchers, we can call that *error-term noise*, and it is not really relevant for the question of when to use an FPF, but it does matter for the general questions of when and whether fixed-price contracts can be used. Better predicting these wage changes could therefore be crucial if FEMA hopes to use fixed-price contracts moving forward.
- **geographic magnitude of a disaster:** One hypothesis is that the larger the disaster area, the likelier it is that there will be a large effect on local aggregate prices. For example,

---

2   Contact the authors for more information.

during the coronavirus disease 2019 (COVID-19) pandemic, states bid against each other for personal protective equipment and ventilators, driving up those products' prices (Livingston, Desai, and Berkwits, 2020). By explicitly modeling the across-county spillover effects of disasters, it might be possible to better predict which disasters will cause large price increases.

- **excess demand for labor or inelastic labor supply for particular skills:** For some disasters, the labor supply for a recovery would come largely from outside a disaster area, and specific job types could face shortages. Certain types of disasters (e.g., high-altitude electromagnetic pulse) can be catastrophic and call for expertise in one field (e.g., skilled electricians), making the labor needed scarce throughout the country and affecting market wages.

- **material and equipment shortages:** The overall magnitude of a recovery effort appears to be less likely to lead to aggregate price increases because there are fewer barriers to the movement of material and equipment than to the movement of workers. That said, there might be specific cases in which the costs of moving material or equipment integral to a disaster recovery could lead to aggregate local price increases. For example, high-altitude electromagnetic pulse events are large in scope and require a great deal of resources to build and transport equipment, such as transformers.

- **housing shortages and transportation delays:** Disaster effects and geography could make it challenging to live near a disaster area (e.g., earthquake and aftershocks, island destroyed by a hurricane) and difficult to work in or to bring in materials and equipment, thereby driving up costs. That said, for the housing and transportation components to directly affect large price changes after a disaster, the recovery effort itself would have to affect supply and demand for housing or transportation. For example, demand for transportation could increase if a vital bridge collapses that cannot be fixed soon after a disaster (because of, e.g., aftershocks, security issues) that could lead to sourcing more-expensive forms of transportation (e.g., helicopters).

- **regional wealth and institutional capacity:** One hypothesis is that greater wealth and institutional capacity might apply downward pressure on price increases after a disaster. The skills, procedures, and organization of the institutions in relatively wealthy areas might be strong enough to start recovery soon after a disaster and maintain a relatively coordinated effort. In small and impoverished communities, limited wealth and institutional capacity might lead to inefficiencies, further driving up costs of a recovery, although these areas might receive support from larger areas with greater capacity. The interaction of city size and poverty measures could be explored.

- **dynamics:** Response and recovery projects can incur large cost overruns from their baselines that lead to subsequent project delays and increased costs.

Simulations

Although the method we developed has theoretical backing, it is unclear, given its novelty, how well it works in practice. We therefore present three simulations meant to study how well the method works and to highlight some limitations.

Assumption 1: A Normally Distributed Effect Distribution

We began with a simulation in which the true effects were assumed to be distributed normally, with a mean of 0 and a standard deviation of 1. The observed change was then the true effect plus an error term, which was also distributed normally with a mean of 0 and standard deviation of 1. The observed change, being the sum of two normal deviates, was therefore also distributed normally. We then simulated a sample of 2,500 observations from this data-generating process. Figure A.1 illustrates the resulting sample, in which the histogram shows the distribution of the unobserved true effects and the blue line shows the distribution of the observed changes.

After simulating the data, we then used the approach described in Chapter Three to estimate the distribution of effects. The results are shown in Figure A.2. The results highlight the promise of the proposed approach; the resulting estimated distribution of effects (the blue line) is nearly identical to the unobserved distribution of true effects (the histogram). Although this is strong support for use of the methodology, the next two examples illustrate some limitations.

FIGURE A.1

Observed Distribution of Disaster Effects and True-Effect Distribution, Assuming Normal Distribution

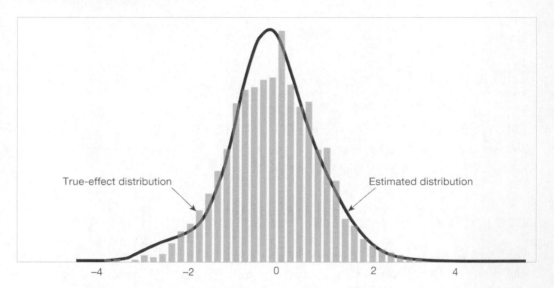

Effect on average construction wage change, as a percentage

NOTE: We assumed that the distribution of true effects was a normal distribution. The histogram shows the true-effect distribution; the observed distribution is shown by the blue line.

FIGURE A.2

Estimated Distribution of Disaster Effects and True-Effect Distribution, Assuming Normal Distribution

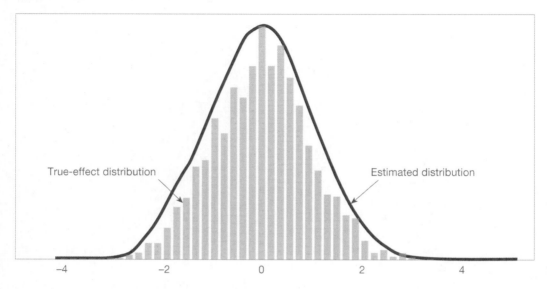

Effect on average construction wage change, as a percentage

NOTE: We assumed that the distribution of true effects was a normal distribution. The histogram shows the true-effect distribution; the observed distribution is shown by the blue line.

Assumption 2: A Uniformly Distributed Effect Distribution

In the next simulation, we assumed that the true effects were distributed uniformly, with the effects ranging from 0 to 3. Like in the previous simulation, we then assumed that the observed change was the true effect plus a normally distributed error term, with a mean of 0 and standard deviation of 1, and simulated a sample of 2,500 observations from this data-generating process. Figure A.3 illustrates the resulting sample, again with the histogram showing the distribution of the unobserved true effects (which we assumed were uniformly distributed) and the blue line showing the distribution of the observed changes.

Applying the method described in Chapter Three gives an estimated-effect distribution shown in Figure A.4. Although the estimated distribution of effects does not align exactly with the true distribution of effects, the approach appears to have been successful for our purposes in two respects:

- The estimated-effect distribution does accurately reflect the fact that the bulk of the effects are between 0 and 3. Going from a normal distribution of observed changes to a distribution that accurately identifies almost all of the true effects between 0 and 3 is an important achievement.

FIGURE A.3

Observed Distribution of Disaster Effects and True-Effect Distribution, Assuming Uniform Distribution

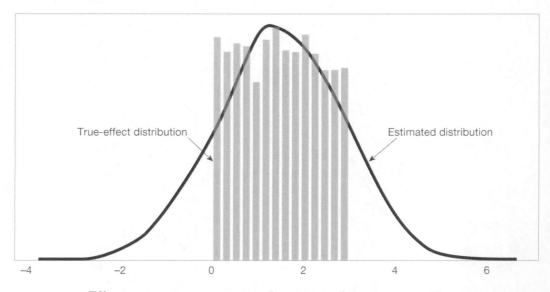

Effect on average construction wage change, percentage

NOTE: We assumed that the distribution of true effects was uniform. The histogram shows the true-effect distribution; the observed distribution is shown by the blue line.

- The estimated-effect distribution is substantially more uniform than a normal distribution would suggest—that is, it appears that the uniform distribution has a smaller variance than the error term, suggesting that the approach was able to separate much of the signal from the noise. That said, the resulting distribution is overly smooth; it overstates the probability of effects being less than 0 or greater than 3 while understating the probability of effects being slightly more than 0 or slightly less than 3. To emphasize the practical implications of this result, we conducted one final simulation, discussed below.

FIGURE A.4

Estimated Distribution of Disaster Effects and True-Effect Distribution, Assuming Uniform Distribution

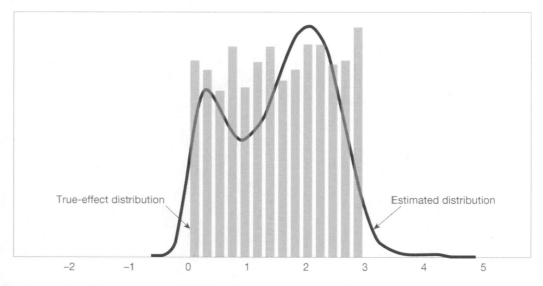

Effect on average construction wage change, as a percentage

NOTE: We assumed that the distribution of true effects was uniform. The histogram shows the true-effect distribution; the observed distribution is shown by the blue line.

Assumption 3: A Right-Skewed Effect Distribution

As our final simulation, we used a true-effect distribution most similar to our prior beliefs about the true distribution of disasters' actual effects on wages. For this, we assumed that the true effect was generated from a mixing distribution, with a 50-percent chance that the true effect would be 0 and a 50-percent chance that the true effect would come from a lognormal distribution with the mean and standard deviation of the underlying normal distribution to be 0 and 1, respectively. Again, we assumed that the observed change was the true effect plus a normally distributed error term, with a mean of 0 and standard deviation of 1, and we then simulated a sample of 2,500 observations from this data-generating process. Figure A.5 illustrates the resulting sample, again with the histogram showing the distribution of the unobserved true effects and the blue line showing the distribution of the observed changes.

The results, shown in Figure A.6, again highlight that the method does well recovering the general shape of the true signal despite the loud noise and accurately captures the long right tail of true effects. The method does not, however, do a great job of determining sharp edges in the true-effect distribution. Practically speaking, this means that a portion of the observations in the study had a negative effect when the true-effect distribution is weakly positive. We think that the "benefits" outweigh the "costs" of this approach yet highlight the need to consider the implications of overly smooth tails when using this methodology.

FIGURE A.5

Observed Distribution of Disaster Effects and True-Effect Distribution, Assuming Right-Skewed Distribution

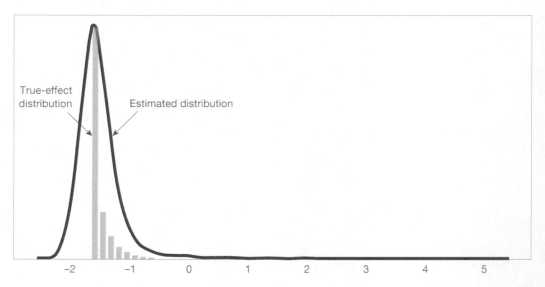

Effect on average construction wage change, as a percentage

NOTE: We assumed that the distribution of true effects was right-skewed. The histogram shows the true-effect distribution; the observed distribution is shown by the blue line.

Thus far, we have separately shown the estimated and observed distributions, with different assumptions about the underlying distribution (i.e., normal, uniform, and right skewed). It is worth noting that the method's inability to determine the sharp edges in the true-effect distribution (in histograms) is not generated by issues with our computational approach, such as not iterating enough or having an insufficient number of grid points, and instead is a problem with identification. This is evident in Figure A.7, which shows the observed distribution of changes under two hypothetical true-effect distributions. The solid blue distribution assumed that the true-effect distribution was indeed equal to the true-effect distribution, and the dashed orange distribution assumed that the true-effect distribution was equal to the estimated-effect distribution. The fact that these two observed distributions are nearly equal suggests that it is nearly impossible to distinguish between the true-effect distribution and estimated-effect distribution from the observed data alone.

Although developing a better understanding of the range of effect distributions consistent with the observed distribution of changes was beyond the scope of this project, it is an interesting theoretical question of practical importance.

FIGURE A.6

Estimated Distribution of Disaster Effects and True-Effect Distribution, Assuming Right-Skewed Distribution

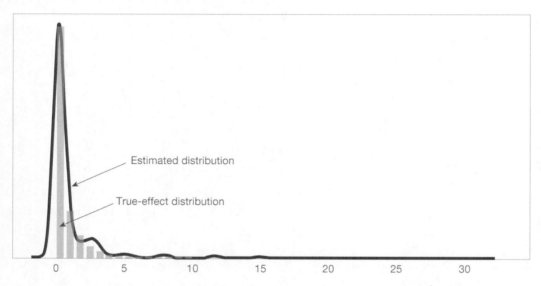

Effect on average construction wage change, as a percentage

NOTE: We assumed that the distribution of true effects was right-skewed. The histogram shows the true-effect distribution; the observed distribution is shown by the blue line.

FIGURE A.7

Comparison of Observed and Implied Distributions

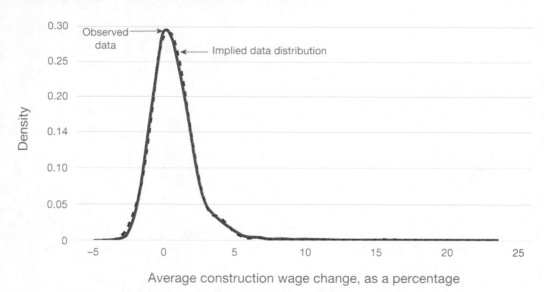

Average construction wage change, as a percentage

NOTE: The observed distribution assumes the true-effect distribution. The implied data distribution assumes the estimated-effect distribution.

Potential Correlates Studied

A County's Poverty

One set of characteristics we analyzed measures how poor a county is before a disaster. One way to measure this is by seeing how the poverty rate in a county affects the likelihood that there will be a large increase in average construction wages postdisaster. This is shown in Figure B.1, which shows some evidence that high-poverty counties are likelier to see increases in average construction wages postdisaster, as evidenced by the high-poverty line generally being above the other lines. This effect is not entirely clear, in that the probabilities of a large average wage increase based on different poverty levels converge and even switch ordering as disaster size increases.

We next split counties into strata using the ratio of their average construction wages predisaster to the U.S. average construction wage predisaster. As shown in Figure B.2, counties

FIGURE B.1

The Relationship Between Per Capita Property Damage and the Probability of a Cost Increase of at Least 10 Percent, by Poverty Group

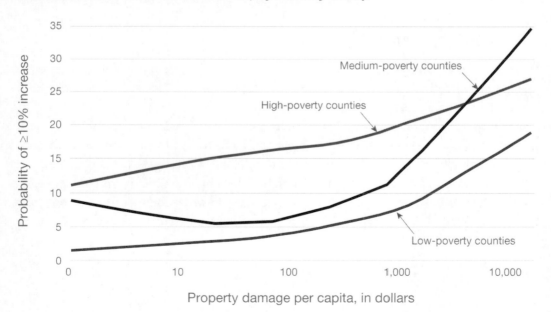

FIGURE B.2

The Relationship Between Per Capita Property Damage and the Probability of a Cost Increase of at Least 10 Percent, by Wage Group

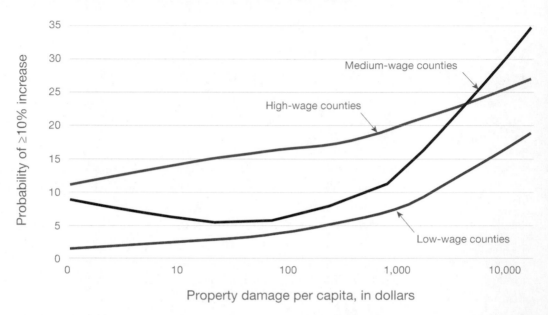

with low average construction wages in the year before the disaster were more likely to see large increases in their average construction wages. However, this relationship is true for all disasters and not just large ones, suggesting that we are insufficiently modeling the counties' wage trends rather than that it is an indicator of heterogeneous treatment effects.

A County's Housing Supply

Finally, many of the scenarios included a discussion of housing availability. Although we could not directly observe how available housing was after a disaster, we determined how expensive housing was in the county before the disaster, under the assumption that high rental prices were indicative of low housing supply. The results are shown in Figure B.3, which suggests that counties with high rent are the least likely to see an increase in their average construction wages postdisaster. One important note is that these counties are likely also the counties with high levels of in-migration, which complicates the interpretation. Furthermore, the relationship between the medium-rent and low-rent counties is more complicated under this classification than when classifying the counties based on their in-migration rates.

FIGURE B.3

The Relationship Between Per Capita Property Damage and the Probability of a Cost Increase of at Least 10 Percent, by Amount of Rent

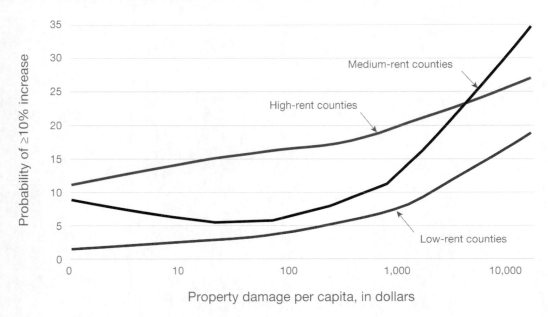

The Threshold Methodology

In Chapter Five, we showed that two criteria—property damage per capita and in-migration rates—were predictive of average construction wage changes due to a disaster. We now explore how well they can together predict whether a disaster will cause increases in average construction wages of more than 10 percent in a county. To do so, we focused on simple rules that set thresholds for the two variables; if a disaster met both thresholds (which together make a criterion), we classified a disaster as being likely to cause construction wage increases of at least 10 percent. We then aimed to calculate how well these thresholds predict large increases.

When setting the threshold, there is a tension between not overpredicting the number of disasters that cause large increases in average wages and not missing disasters that do cause large average wage increases. To describe this trade-off, we estimate the positive rate (PR) and true PR (TPR) for various potential thresholds. The PR is the total percentage of disasters predicted to cause increases in average wages of at least 10 percent. The TPR, also known as the sensitivity of the classification, is the fraction of PR with observed increases in average wages of at least 10 percent.

A significant challenge in this is that we cannot actually observe whether a disaster causes increases in average wages of at least 10 percent, which we need for the numerator of the TPR. To get around this issue, we combined the distribution of estimated effects presented in Figure 4.1 in Chapter Four with the observed percentage change in average wages to estimate a posterior distribution of impacts for each disaster. To do so, we used Bayes's law, which states that, for any potential impact T,

$$\Pr\left(\tau = T \mid \Delta y_{i,t}\right) = \frac{\Pr\left(\Delta y_{i,t} \mid \tau = T\right)\Pr\left(\tau = T\right)}{\Pr\left(\Delta y_{i,t}\right)}.$$

Figure 3.1 in Chapter Three provides the estimate of $\Pr\left(\tau = T\right)$, and the assumption of a normally distributed error term gives an estimate of $\Pr\left(\Delta y_{i,t} \mid \tau = T\right)$. We could then estimate the posterior $\Pr\left(\tau = T \mid \Delta y_{i,t}\right)$ using the constraint that

$$\sum \Pr\left(\tau = T \mid \Delta y_{i,t}\right) = 1.$$

Given the posterior distribution, we could then calculate the probability that the disaster would increase average wages by more than 10 percent, by calculating $\sum_{T>.1} \Pr\left(\tau = T \mid \Delta y_{i,t}\right)$, which we denote as $\Pr_{i,t}$.

Given the posterior probability estimates, we could define the TPR as

$$\frac{\sum_{\forall i,t} \Pr_{i,t} * Predicted_{i,t}}{\sum_{\forall i,t} \Pr_{i,t}},$$

where $Predicted_{i,t}$ equals 1 if we predict that the county-disaster indexed by (i,t) had a 10-percent increase in wages due to the disaster. With complete information, $\Pr_{i,t}$ would be either 0 or 1 and this would be identical to the traditional TPR measures.

We calculated the positive rate as

$$PR = \frac{\sum_{\forall i,t} Predicted_{i,t}}{\sum_{\forall i,t} 1}.$$

Note that, although Bayes's law allowed us to calculate the TPR and PR, the fact that we cannot directly observe whether a county-disaster indexed by (i,t) actually had a 10-percent increase in average wages due to the disaster and instead could estimate only that $\Pr_{i,t}$ does cause some issues in estimating the TPR. Most notably, the fact that there is noise in our classifications biases the curve toward what we would get with random guessing.

Estimated Coefficients

As part of the method, we estimated how county covariates related to average construction wage changes in the county-years unaffected by a disaster. The parameter estimates are reported in Table D.1.

TABLE D.1

Ordinary-Least-Squares Regression Estimates of τ and β

Characteristic	τ	β
Employment size	8,869.0635**	8,869.0635**
	(191.412)	(8.183)
Mobility (average, in total)	14.2979**	0.1482**
	(1.101)	(0.047)
Mobility (average, in a different state)	−7.8004**	−0.4223**
	(1.452)	(0.062)
Unemployment rate	273.3083**	−15.7279**
	(43.608)	(1.864)
Construction labor pool, as a percentage of all workers	−43.1438	29.5524**
	(42.431)	(1.814)
Poverty rate (Small Area Income and Poverty Estimates)	363.2608**	12.1478**
	(18.231)	(0.779)
Wage ratio	50.1415**	−11.6194**
	(5.139)	(0.22)
Rent ratio	−84.6996**	8.8003**
	(6.029)	(0.258)
Number of observations	46,595	46,595
R^2	0.25	0.083

NOTE: ** = $p < .05$. *** = $p < .01$. Standard errors are in parentheses and do not account for potential spatial or intertemporal autocorrelation.

The Stress-Testing Method, Data, and Results

The Method

The core CGE model considers a variety of economic entities in each jurisdiction, including the government, households, and firms. The economic behavior and interactions of each entity are modeled using standard preference functional forms, based on established microeconomic theory and computational methods. The model is numerically simulated using the computer program General Algebraic Modeling System and its mathematical programming system for general equilibrium solver.

We assumed that each jurisdiction could trade with other jurisdictions around the world but that each was too small to affect world prices or incomes (i.e., small open economy). We assumed that each was hit with a disaster and received a series of expenditures over time using historical obligations from PA spending. Then, each firm selected the combination of labor, goods, and service inputs required to produce its output of goods and services and maximize its profits. Households maximize their utility by consuming goods and services and saving from their income received for working at firms and rental income from assets. The model finds the equilibrium at which prices of all goods and services are such that the quantity supplied equals the quantity demanded across all sectors (e.g., construction, agriculture, services). We note that in-migration rates of each jurisdiction were not explicitly incorporated in the calibration; however, location-specific in-migration can arise through the interactions with the outside world through trade.

Our main result of interest for this work is a price index consisting of four specific price variables:

- the wage rate
- the rental rate of capital, as a proxy for the price of equipment
- the price of manufactured goods, as a proxy for the price of materials
- the average price of construction.

The rental rate of capital and the price of manufactured goods were combined to generate a price index, or the FPF.

In sum, we

1. constructed a series of expenditure time paths
2. shocked the economy with one year of spending
3. allowed households, firms, and governments to interact to calculate equilibrium
4. updated labor and capital stocks based on wage and rental rates
5. repeated this process for the entire spending path.

Constructing a Series of Expenditure Time Paths

The expenditure plans are developed across all categories of permanent work for PA. Thus, four construction sectors correspond to PA, and an outside construction sector was used for all other construction. We used the stochastic expenditure simulator from the work of Strong and his colleagues (Strong, Wenger, Anderson, Edwards, Muggy, et al., 2019a; Strong, Wenger, Anderson, Edwards, Muggy, et al., 2019b; Strong, Wenger, Anderson, Edwards, and Siler-Evans, 2019; Strong, Wenger, Opper, et al., 2019) on estimating an FPF and normalized it to the appropriate aggregate expenditure level. Given the uncertainty in expenditure paths, we iterated 100 expenditure scenarios for each jurisdiction. In the "Results" section of this appendix, we report the mean, median, 75th-percentile, and 90th-percentile results for construction costs within the first three years across 100 iterations.

Scenario Jurisdiction Description

Figure E.1 illustrates the cross-section of jurisdictions in terms of low in-migration (less than 2.5 percent) to high (more than 2.5 percent) and low GRP (less than or equal to $45 billion in FY 2018 dollars) to high (more than $45 billion in FY 2018 dollars). The red rectangle indicates the jurisdictions with low in-migration that are therefore more likely in need of an FPF if damage exceeds $10,000 per capita. Jurisdictions on the right-hand side have high in-migration and are therefore less likely to meet the criterion for an FPF estimation.

The Data

The model's equations are calibrated to each jurisdiction using the social accounting matrix (SAM) provided in IMPLAN for 2018.[1] A SAM is a table expressed in terms of incomes and expenditures (i.e., a double-entry accounting method), which is now a standard approach to calibrate functional form to real-life data.

---

[1] Implicitly, we assumed that the underlying structure of the economy was unchanged by the disaster, which might not be appropriate for large-scale disruptions. But we do not have a systematic approach for destroying sector-specific capital stocks or migration patterns following storms. As a result, we adopted the 2018 SAM as a decent approximation for all areas.

FIGURE E.1

Categorization of Jurisdictions Selected for Stress Testing

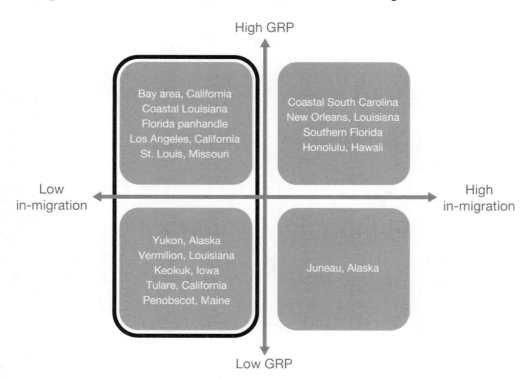

Results

In Table E.1, we present the construction price results for disaster-recovery spending of $1,000 per capita and $10,000 per capita (in FY 2018 U.S. dollars). For each jurisdiction, we provide the price effects at the mean, median, 75th-percentile, and 90th-percentile ranges of results across the 100 iterations. Results show that spending $1,000 per capita on damage yields an FPF of 1.0 for all jurisdictions. This matches our hypothesis that no jurisdiction with this level of damage would require an FPF estimate.

Regarding spending of $10,000 per capita, none of the low– or high–in-migration jurisdictions yields an FPF estimate of 1.10 or greater. We hypothesized FPF estimates of 1.10 or greater for three of the 11 low–in-migration jurisdictions and no high–in-migration areas. Therefore, the criteria were accurate for high–in-migration jurisdictions but not low in-migration. That said, we see a pattern in which areas with low in-migration are more likely than those with high in-migration to have FPF estimates greater than 1.0, especially when considering the upper-quartile FPF estimates (i.e., depending on the expenditure path). This is suggestive that the in-migration criteria are indeed a useful measure even though we have not directly incorporated them into the modeling effort. This could arise through the interactions with the outside world through trade.

TABLE E.1

Construction Price Relative to Baseline for $1,000 and $10,000 Per Capita in Damage, in Fiscal Year 2018 U.S. Dollars

| | $1,000 Per Capita in Damage | | | | $10,000 Per Capita in Damage | | | |
| | | | Percentile | | | | Percentile | |
Jurisdiction	Mean	Median	75th	90th	Mean	Median	75th	90th
Low in-migration								
Bay area, California	1.00	1.00	1.00	1.00	1.00	1.00	1.00	1.00
Coastal Louisiana	1.00	1.00	1.00	1.00	1.00	1.00	1.00	1.00
Florida panhandle	1.00	1.00	1.00	1.00	1.00	1.00	1.00	**1.01**
Keokuk, Iowa	1.00	1.00	1.00	1.00	**1.01**	1.00	**1.01**	**1.01**
Los Angeles, California	1.00	1.00	1.00	1.00	1.00	1.00	1.00	1.00
Maine	1.00	1.00	1.00	1.00	1.00	1.00	**1.01**	**1.01**
Penobscot, Maine	1.00	1.00	1.00	1.00	**1.01**	1.00	**1.01**	**1.02**
Saint Louis, Missouri	1.00	1.00	1.00	1.00	1.00	1.00	**1.01**	**1.01**
Tulare, California	1.00	1.00	1.00	1.00	1.00	1.00	1.00	1.00
Vermillion, Louisiana	1.00	1.00	1.00	1.00	1.00	1.00	**1.01**	**1.01**
Yukon, Alaska	1.00	1.00	1.00	1.00	**1.03**	**1.03**	**1.04**	**1.05**
High in-migration								
Coastal South Carolina	1.00	1.00	1.00	1.00	1.00	1.00	1.00	1.00
Honolulu, Hawaii	1.00	1.00	1.00	1.00	1.00	1.00	1.00	1.00
Juneau, Alaska	1.00	1.00	1.00	1.00	1.00	1.00	**1.01**	**1.01**
New Orleans, Louisiana	1.00	1.00	1.00	1.00	1.00	1.00	1.00	**1.01**
Southern Florida	1.00	1.00	1.00	1.00	1.00	1.00	1.00	**1.01**

NOTE: Bold indicates an estimate greater than 1.00.

Regarding tests with more damage, Table E.2 displays the size of the disaster in terms of percentage and of amount per capita, along with FPF estimate results at the mean and 50th to 90th percentiles for each scenario and jurisdiction. Out of 11 low–in-migration areas, we found mean FPF estimates of 1.10 or greater for one (scenario 1) and four (scenario 2) areas. When considering the upper-quartile estimates (and thus different spend paths) of scenario 2, we found FPF estimates greater than 1.10 for more than 50 percent (six of 11) of low–in-migration areas. Out of five high–in-migration areas, we found mean FPF estimates of 1.10 or greater for none of the areas in scenario 1 and four of the five areas in scenario 2. Indeed, in the four areas with FPF estimates greater than 1.10, a disaster the economic size of Hurricane Katrina would cost 88 percent to 145 percent of their GRPs; in the fifth, a hurricane this size would cause damage of 28 percent of GRP (or approximately $16,000 per capita).

TABLE E.2
Construction Prices Relative to Baseline for Larger Disasters

| | Scenario 1 Disaster ($50 billion or 50% of GRP) | | | | Scenario 2 Disaster ($81 billion or 100% of GRP) | | | |
| | Size of Damage | | FPF Estimate | | Size of Damage | | FPF Estimate | |
Jurisdiction	Percentage of GRP	Dollars Per Capita	Value	50th–90th Percentiles	Percentage of GRP	Dollars Per Capita	Value	50th–90th Percentiles
Low in-migration								
Los Angeles, California	4	2,665	1.00	1.00–1.00	7	4,317	1.00	1.00–1.00
Bay area, California	5	6,449	1.00	1.00–1.01	8	10,448	1.00	1.00–1.01
Coastal Louisiana	35	20,915	1.01	1.00–1.02	57	33,882	1.03	1.02–1.09
Saint Louis, Missouri	36	20,526	1.01	1.01–1.03	58	33,253	1.05	1.02–**1.14**
Penobscot, Maine	50	21,192	1.03	1.02–1.08	100	42,384	1.10	1.07–**1.24**
Keokuk, Iowa	50	14,670	1.01	1.01–1.02	100	29,340	1.02	1.01–1.06
Tulare, California	50	19,140	1.01	1.00–1.04	100	38,280	1.07	1.03–**1.21**
Vermillion, Louisiana	50	13,371	1.01	1.00–1.02	100	26,742	1.03	1.02–1.09
Yukon, Alaska	50	31,913	1.11	1.07–**1.26**	100	63,826	1.35	1.15–1.99
Maine	77	37,358	1.06	1.04–**1.17**	125	60,520	1.14	1.09–**1.35**
Florida panhandle	106	46,201	1.06	1.03–**1.15**	172	74,846	1.14	1.10–1.34
High in-migration								
Southern Florida	17	9,678	1.00	1.00–1.01	28	15,678	1.01	1.00–1.02
Juneau, Alaska	50	31,140	1.02	1.01–1.06	100	62,280	1.10	1.04–**1.28**
New Orleans, Louisiana	54	34,465	1.04	1.02–**1.12**	88	55,833	1.11	1.07–**1.26**
Honolulu, Hawaii	70	51,020	1.09	1.07–**1.20**	114	82,653	1.19	1.14–1.42
Coastal South Carolina	89	48,544	1.09	1.06–**1.23**	145	78,642	1.21	1.14–1.48

NOTE: Bold indicates an estimate of 1.10 or greater.

Figure 6.3 in Chapter Six plots all the mean FPF estimates by damage per capita, for low–in-migration (blue dots) and high–in-migration (red *x*'s) locations. We found that a scenario with damage of less than $10,000 per capita has an FPF of 1.0. At $10,000 per capita, we started to observe greater variation in FPF estimates, with jurisdictions ranging from 1.00 to 1.04. Beyond $55,000 per capita in damage, mean FPF estimates are always greater than 1.10. The trend lines for the low–in-migration locations (blue dotted line) and high–in-migration locations (red dashed line) suggest that prices increase by more in low–in-migration areas for all levels of damage.

In all situations, Yukon, Alaska, was the outlier in terms of the FPF. At approximately $32,000 per capita in damage (50 percent of GRP), Yukon has the highest FPF, at approximately 1.11. When we increased damage in Yukon to approximately $64,000 in per capita (100 percent of GRP), the FPF mean estimate increased to 1.35. The next closest in that range of per capita damage is coastal South Carolina (FPF = 1.21), which would take an economic disaster of 145 percent of its GRP or nearly $80,000 per capita in damage. The capital-to-labor ratio in Yukon is approximately 0.83. For most of the other communities, this ratio is closer to 0.9 or above. Although we have not considered the intercounty trade effects, we have aggregated counties in an attempt to think about the most appropriate area for a market. For more-rural communities, that is a single county.

In the low-GRP areas, although we shocked all the communities with the same level of damage (i.e., 50 percent and 100 percent of their GRPs), they responded with different price effects. In part, this is because they differ in terms of relative integration in the broader national economy and therefore react differently to the expenditure shock. An implication of these results is that such places as Yukon–Koyukuk, Alaska; Penobscot, Maine; and Juneau, Alaska, are likely to require an FPF estimate for large PA disasters.

Within-Laborshed Analysis of Property Damage and Wage Increases

As discussed in Chapter Two, we chose to conduct the analysis at the county-year level rather than a more aggregated level, such as the economic areas defined by BEA. In doing so, we ignored the potentially important effect of a large disaster on the neighboring counties' construction wages. However, conducting the analysis at a more aggregated level risks missing meaningful increases in construct costs that occur in the affected counties but do not occur in the rest of the laborshed. If that occurs, aggregating to the laborshed-year level risks missing more-localized effects, which could affect the cost of rebuilding.

A natural way to test whether the laborshed-year level would be overaggregating the data is to look within laborshed-years at the relationship between disaster size and construction wage changes. Specifically, we conducted the test by restricting our analysis to laborshed-years, where we used BEA's economic areas to define the laborshed, in which at least one county had $1,000 in per capita property damage due to disasters in that year. We then use the methods defined in Chapter Three of this report to estimate the effect of disasters on construction wages in each county of the laborshed for that year. Finally, we ran a regression of the construction wage effects in each county on the log per capita property damage in the county caused by disasters in the year along with laborshed-by-year fixed effects. Thus, the regression controls for laborshedwide changes in construction wages in the year, some of which could be due to the disaster.

As shown in Table F.1, even within laborshed-years, counties with more property damage have larger wage increases. This suggests that aggregating the analysis to the laborshed-year level would cause us to underestimate the disasters' true effect on construction wages in the counties that are hit particularly hard by the disaster, which are precisely the counties on which we focused in this study. We therefore opted to conduct the analysis at the county-year level rather than a more aggregated level.

TABLE F.1

Within–Laborshed-Year Relationship Between Disaster Impacts and Construction Wage Changes

Measure	Construction Wage Change
Log property damage per capita	0.105*
	(0.061)
Number of observations	3,293
R^2	0.22

NOTE: * = p < .1. ** = p < .05. *** = p < .01. Standard errors, in parentheses, are clustered at the county level and do not account for potential spatial autocorrelations. The regression includes economic area–by-year fixed effects. The dependent variable is the mean of the posterior distribution of wage changes due to disasters; Chapter Three has more details on how the dependent variable is constructed.

Abbreviations

ACS	American Community Survey
BEA	Bureau of Economic Analysis
CEF	Cost Estimating Format
CGE	computable general equilibrium
FEMA	Federal Emergency Management Agency
FPF	future price forecast
FY	fiscal year
GRP	gross regional product
IRS	Internal Revenue Service
PA	Public Assistance
PR	positive rate
SAM	social accounting matrix
SHELDUS	Spatial Hazard Events and Losses Database for the United States
TPR	true positive rate
USVI	U.S. Virgin Islands

References

Abe, Naohito, Chiaki Moriguchi, and Noriko Inakura, *The Effects of Natural Disasters on Prices and Purchasing Behaviors: The Case of the Great East Japan Earthquake*, Hitotsubashi University, Institute of Economic Research, Research Center for Economic and Social Risks, Discussion Paper 14-1, September 10, 2014. As of July 18, 2021:
https://ideas.repec.org/p/hit/rcesrs/dp14-1.html

Belasen, Ariel R., and Solomon W. Polachek, "How Hurricanes Affect Wages and Employment in Local Labor Markets," *American Economic Review*, Vol. 98, No. 2, May 2008, pp. 49–53.

Bonhomme, Stéphane, and Jean-Marc Robin, "Generalized Non-Parametric Deconvolution with an Application to Earnings Dynamics," *Review of Economic Studies*, Vol. 77, No. 2, April 2010, pp. 491–533.

Botzen, W. J. Wouter, Olivier Deschenes, and Mark Sanders, "The Economic Impacts of Natural Disasters: A Review of Models and Empirical Studies," *Review of Environmental Economics and Policy*, Vol. 13, No. 2, 2019, pp. 167–188. As of July 18, 2021:
https://www.journals.uchicago.edu/doi/abs/10.1093/reep/rez004

Boustan, Leah Platt, Matthew E. Kahn, Paul W. Rhode, and Maria Lucia Yanguas, "The Effect of Natural Disasters on Economic Activity in US Counties: A Century of Data," *Journal of Urban Economics*, Vol. 118, July 2020, art. 103257.

Cavallo, Alberto, Eduardo Cavallo, and Roberto Rigobon, "Prices and Supply Disruptions During Natural Disasters," *Review of Income and Wealth*, Vol. 60, No. S2, November 2014, pp. S449–S471.

Center for Emergency Management and Homeland Security, Arizona State University, "Metadata," webpage, undated. As of July 20, 2021:
https://cemhs.asu.edu/node/7

Code of Federal Regulations, Title 2, Grants and Agreements; Subtitle A, Office of Management and Budget Guidance for Grants and Agreements; Chapter II, Office of Management and Budget Guidance; Part 200, Uniform Administrative Requirements, Cost Principles, and Audit Requirements for Federal Awards. As of August 24, 2021:
https://www.ecfr.gov/cgi-bin/text-idx?tpl=/ecfrbrowse/Title02/2cfr200_main_02.tpl

Deryugina, Tatyana, Laura Kawano, and Steven Levitt, "The Economic Impact of Hurricane Katrina on Its Victims: Evidence from Individual Tax Returns," *American Economic Journal: Applied Economics*, Vol. 10, No. 2, April 2018, pp. 202–233. As of July 18, 2021:
https://www.aeaweb.org/articles?id=10.1257/app.20160307

Federal Emergency Management Agency, U.S. Department of Homeland Security, "Procurement Under Grants: Under Exigent or Emergency Circumstances," news release, Washington, D.C., March 20, 2020a. As of July 18, 2021:
https://www.fema.gov/news-release/20200514/
procurement-under-grants-under-exigent-or-emergency-circumstances

———, *FEMA Preliminary Damage Assessment Guide*, Washington, D.C., May 28, 2020b. As of December 16, 2020:
https://www.fema.gov/disaster/how-declared/preliminary-damage-assessments/guide

———, *Public Assistance Program and Policy Guide*, version 4, Washington, D.C., FP 104-009-2, effective June 1, 2020c. As of July 18, 2021:
https://www.fema.gov/assistance/public/policy-guidance-fact-sheets

FEMA—*See* Federal Emergency Management Agency.

Feng, Long, and Lee H. Dicker, "Approximate Nonparametric Maximum Likelihood for Mixture Models: A Convex Optimization Approach to Fitting Arbitrary Multivariate Mixing Distributions," *Computational Statistics and Data Analysis*, Vol. 122, June 2018, pp. 80–91.

Gonzalez, Gabriella C., Kathryn A. Edwards, Melanie A. Zaber, Megan Andrew, Aaron Strong, and Craig A. Bond, *Supporting a 21st-Century Workforce in Puerto Rico: Challenges and Options for Improving Puerto Rico's Workforce System Following Hurricanes Irma and Maria in 2017*, Homeland Security Operational Analysis Center operated by the RAND Corporation, RR-2856-DHS, 2020. As of July 18, 2021:
https://www.rand.org/pubs/research_reports/RR2856.html

Groen, Jeffrey A., Mark J. Kutzbach, and Anne E. Polivka, "Storms and Jobs: The Effect of Hurricanes on Individuals' Employment and Earnings over the Long Term," *Journal of Labor Economics*, Vol. 38, No. 3, July 2020, pp. 653–685.

Huerta-Wong, Juan Enrique, Julieth Santamaria, Adan Silverio-Murillo, and Isidro Soloaga, *The Effect of Natural Disasters on Consumption and Prices: Evidence from Mexico*, December 17, 2018. As of July 18, 2021:
https://www.juliethsantamaria.com/s/Consumption-prices-disasters.pdf

Hunt, P., K. Klima, S. Cohen, S. McKenna, and R. Briggs, *Exploring Criteria for When to Apply a Future Price Forecast*, Homeland Security Operational Analysis Center operated by the RAND Corporation, unpublished, 2020.

Internal Revenue Service, "SOI Tax Stats: Migration Data," webpage, last updated May 25, 2021. As of July 18, 2021:
https://www.irs.gov/statistics/soi-tax-stats-migration-data

IRS—*See* Internal Revenue Service.

Kiefer, J., and J. Wolfowitz, "Consistency of the Maximum Likelihood Estimator in the Presence of Infinitely Many Incidental Parameters," *Annals of Mathematical Statistics*, Vol. 27, No. 4, December 1956, pp. 887–906.

Koenker, Roger, and Ivan Mizera, "Convex Optimization, Shape Constraints, Compound Decisions, and Empirical Bayes Rules," *Journal of the American Statistical Association*, Vol. 109, No. 506, June 2014, pp. 674–685.

Laird, Nan, "Nonparametric Maximum Likelihood Estimation of a Mixing Distribution," *Journal of the American Statistical Association*, Vol. 73, No. 364, December 1978, pp. 805–811.

Livingston, Edward, Angel Desai, and Michael Berkwits, "Sourcing Personal Protective Equipment During the COVID-19 Pandemic," *JAMA*, Vol. 323, No. 19, March 28, 2020, pp. 1912–1914.

Murphy, Anthony, and Eric Strobl, *The Impact of Hurricanes on Housing Prices: Evidence from U.S. Coastal Cities*, Federal Reserve Bank of Dallas, Research Department, Working Paper 1009, October 2010. As of July 18, 2021:
https://www.dallasfed.org/~/media/documents/research/papers/2010-1.html

Public Law 93-288, Disaster Relief Act of 1974, May 22, 1974. As of November 7, 2020:
https://www.hsdl.org/?abstract&did=458661

Public Law 107-296, Homeland Security Act of 2002, November 25, 2002. As of May 12, 2019:
https://www.govinfo.gov/app/details/PLAW-107publ296

Public Law 113-2, an act making supplemental appropriations for the fiscal year ending September 30, 2013, to improve and streamline disaster assistance for Hurricane Sandy, and for other purposes, January 29, 2013. As of November 7, 2020:
https://www.govinfo.gov/app/details/PLAW-113publ2

Strong, A., J. B. Wenger, D. M. Anderson, K. A. Edwards, L. Muggy, and R. Briggs, *An Evaluation of the U.S. Virgin Islands City Cost Index (CCI) and Future Price Forecasts for Construction*, Homeland Security Operational Analysis Center operated by the RAND Corporation, unpublished, 2019a.

———, *An Evaluation of the U.S. Virgin Islands City Cost Index and Future Price Forecast: Addendum*, Homeland Security Operational Analysis Center operated by the RAND Corporation, unpublished, 2019b.

Strong, A., J. B. Wenger, D. M. Anderson, K. A. Edwards, and K. Siler-Evans, *Review and Validation of a FEMA Cost Estimation Approach for FEMA-DR-4339: Future Price Forecast for Puerto Rico*, Homeland Security Operational Analysis Center operated by the RAND Corporation, unpublished, 2019.

Strong, A., J. B. Wenger, I. Opper, D. M. Anderson, K. A. Edwards, K. Siler-Evans, and R. Briggs, *Review and Validation of a FEMA Cost Estimation Approach for FEMA-DR-4339: Future Price Forecast for Puerto Rico: Addendum*, Homeland Security Operational Analysis Center operated by the RAND Corporation, unpublished, 2019.

U.S. Bureau of Labor Statistics, U.S. Department of Labor, *Handbook of Methods*, undated. As of July 20, 2021:
https://www.bls.gov/opub/hom/about.htm

———, "Quarterly Census of Employment and Wages: Overview," last modified August 18, 2021. As of August 25, 2021:
https://www.bls.gov/opub/hom/cew/

U.S. Census Bureau, *American Community Survey: Design and Methodology Report*, version 2.0, Washington, D.C., January 30, 2014. As of July 18, 2021:
https://www.census.gov/programs-surveys/acs/methodology/design-and-methodology.html

———, *Island Areas: Industry Series: Comparative Statistics by Construction Industry for Puerto Rico: 2012 and 2007*, 2015.

———, "2012 Construction (NAICS Sector 23)," webpage, last revised March 30, 2020. As of December 16, 2020:
https://www.census.gov/data/tables/2012/econ/census/construction.html

U.S. Code, Title 6, Domestic Security; Chapter 1, Homeland Security Organization; Subchapter III, Science and Technology in Support of Homeland Security; Section 185, Federally Funded Research and Development Centers. As of March 20, 2021:
https://uscode.house.gov/view.xhtml?req=(title:6%20section:185%20edition:prelim)

U.S. Code, Title 42, The Public Health and Welfare; Chapter 68, Disaster Relief; Subchapter IV, Major Disaster Assistance Programs, Section 5189f, Public Assistance Program Alternative Procedures. As of November 7, 2020:
https://uscode.house.gov/view.xhtml?req=(title:42%20section:5189f%20edition:prelim)

U.S. Government Accountability Office, *Disaster Cost Estimates: FEMA Can Improve Its Learning from Past Experience and Management of Disaster-Related Resources*, Washington, D.C., GAO-08-301, February 22, 2008. As of July 18, 2021:
https://www.gao.gov/products/gao-08-301

Wooldridge, Jeffrey M., *Econometric Analysis of Cross Section and Panel Data*, Cambridge, Mass.: MIT Press, 2010.